Expatriate Tax Manual

Expatriate Tax Manual

Second edition

Colin Cretton, MA, ATII
Principal, KPMG Peat Marwick

Butterworths
London, Dublin & Edinburgh
1991

United Kingdom	Butterworth & Co (Publishers) Ltd, 88 Kingsway, LONDON WC2B 6AB and 4 Hill Street, EDINBURGH EH2 3JZ
Australia	Butterworths Pty Ltd, SYDNEY, MELBOURNE, BRISBANE, ADELAIDE, PERTH, CANBERRA and HOBART
Canada	Butterworths Canada Ltd, TORONTO and VANCOUVER
Ireland	Butterworth (Ireland) Ltd, DUBLIN
Malaysia	Malayan Law Journal Sdn Bhd, KUALA LUMPUR
New Zealand	Butterworths of New Zealand Ltd, WELLINGTON and AUCKLAND
Puerto Rico	Equity de Puerto Rico, Inc, HATO REY
Singapore	Malayan Law Journal Pte Ltd, SINGAPORE
USA	Butterworth Legal Publishers, AUSTIN, Texas; BOSTON, Massachusetts; CLEARWATER, Florida (D & S Publishers); ORFORD, New Hampshire (Equity Publishing); ST PAUL, Minnesota; and SEATTLE, Washington

A CIP Catalogue record for this book is available from the British Library.

First edition 1985

ISBN 0 406 00204 5

Index compiled by Indexing Specialists,
202 Church Road, Hove, East Sussex, BN3 2DJ
Typeset by Colset Pte Ltd., Singapore
Printed and bound in Great Britain by
Biddles, Guildford and Kings Lynn

Foreword

The purpose of this book is to explain in clear, practical terms the UK tax rules affecting individuals, wherever resident, whose investments or employment involve crossing fiscal frontiers. Those whose tax affairs involve the international dimension – expatriates – will often be adept at coping with the tribulations of international travel, the arcane bureaucracy of visas and work permits, or the ground rules of personal investment in a country which is not their own. Expatriates who have to move house face the often frustrating search for a place to live. Even for a limited stay, family life and routines are invariably disrupted, and adjusting to a new living and working environment is always a demanding process.

To an extent, all of the problems mentioned are relatively concrete ones. Most people are aware of them from the outset and are generally equipped to cope without special training or expertise. However, the tax effects of working or living abroad often receive less attention than they deserve, and this is in part because their consequences are not immediately visible. The ever-increasing complexity of the tax rules is itself a disincentive to come to grips with them until all of the expatriate's 'practical' problems have been dealt with. Yet the price of failing to plan effectively for tax can be a high one. Even if valuable tax reliefs are not irrevocably lost, much time and money may have to be spent unscrambling existing arrangements in order to restore the optimum tax position.

The UK tax system is more intricate than most in the field of international personal taxation. The foreign element is superimposed on the already complex personal tax system of income tax (with its Schedules and Cases), capital gains tax and inheritance tax. The interplay of three crucial concepts – residence, ordinary residence and domicile – affects not only territorial scope but also the basis of assessment and entitlement to tax reliefs, as well as a number of other, related issues. The position is further complicated where there is exposure to tax outside the UK, since this can affect the individual's UK tax liabilities. The purely domestic tax law of the UK and the other country may in turn be modified by the provisions of an applicable double taxation agreement between the two states. Although many of the regulatory barriers to personal financial freedom within the EC should have been removed by the end of 1992, the personal tax systems of the member states will remain unharmonised, both as to rates and to tax base. EC residents working or investing in other member states must therefore still rely on the various bilateral tax treaties for relief from double taxation. All of these considerations are as much of relevance to the individual leaving the UK to work or reside abroad as they are to the foreign expatriate visiting the UK.

Because expatriate taxation is a practical problem area, encompassing many different taxes, it can often be difficult and time consuming for practitioners to research their advice in this field if they do not deal with expatriate clients on a day-to-day basis. This book therefore provides a comprehensive, practical guide to the UK tax rules affecting expatriates, bringing together in a single place the various strands within the subject. A working knowledge of the various taxes affecting individuals in the UK is assumed throughout. To enhance the usefulness of the work to practitioners and students alike, the text is fully referenced to source material, including court decisions, statutes and published Inland Revenue statements. For the sake of completeness, the main aspects of the social security regulations and requirements as to visas, residence permits and work permits, have also been mentioned where relevant. The law is stated as at 1 August 1991.

The contents of this book are intended as a general guide to law and practice within the area covered, and not as a substitute for professional advice based on the detailed facts and circumstances of any particular situation. Needless to say, nothing in the book is to be construed as the giving of investment advice within the meaning of the Financial Services Act 1986.

I am grateful to my colleague Peter Nightingale, of KPMG Peat Marwick International Executive Taxation Services, for reviewing the text of the book and making many useful comments and suggestions. Any remaining errors or shortcomings are, naturally, my responsibility. The views expressed are not necessarily those of KPMG Peat Marwick.

Colin Cretton
August 1991

Contents

Contents

Table of statutes

Table of cases

1 UK personal taxation: the foreign element

1.1 The UK system of personal taxation is undeniably a subject of great complexity. Not only are there a number of separate taxes imposed upon individuals, but many of the tax codes have developed piecemeal over a lengthy period of time – about a century and a half in the case of income tax. This work focuses on one aspect of personal taxation, the international dimension, the importance of which has grown markedly in recent years with ever-increasing levels of cross-frontier trade and investment.

1.2 The aim here is to provide a readable, practical guide to the tax rules and the problem areas, and to suggest ways around the obstacles. Comprehensive analysis of each of the taxes involved is outside the present scope, which is instead to highlight those features of the UK tax code which impinge specifically upon personal financial transactions having a foreign element. The subject matter therefore includes not only the tax implications for UK residents investing, working or moving abroad, but also the treatment of non-UK individuals investing in the UK or relocating for employment, business or personal reasons.

1.3 In this chapter, the ground rules of UK international tax for individuals are explained. The concepts of residence and domicile will be examined in greater detail in the two succeeding chapters, before turning to consider specific problem areas. Reference to statutes, decided cases and other published material is made wherever possible, in the hope that the usefulness of the work to practitioners and students will thereby be enhanced.

Basis of taxation

1.4 Two factors central to the taxation of individuals in the UK are residence and domicile. Each of these important concepts is complex and is explained at length in chapters 2 and 3, respectively. The ways in which an individual's residence and domicile status affect his liability to UK tax differ according to the particular tax concerned. For income tax, residence is crucial, because it determines the scope of the individual's liability. An individual who is resident in the UK is subject to income tax on all his sources of income, worldwide. A non-resident, however, is taxable only in respect of income arising from sources in the UK. The reference period for measuring income – the tax year – is in both cases the year ending on 5 April.

1.5 The implications of residence are somewhat different in the case of capital gains tax (CGT). A UK resident is subject to CGT on gains from the

1

disposal of any asset, wherever situated: CGTA 1979 s 2(1). Liability also extends to a non-resident individual who is nevertheless ordinarily resident in the UK (see **2.11**). In contrast with the position for income tax, however, an individual who is neither resident nor ordinarily resident in the UK is not subject to CGT, even if the asset concerned is situated in the UK. Like many tax rules, the latter has exceptions, namely:

(a) where the asset concerned is used in connection with a trade carried on in the UK through a branch: CGTA 1979 s 12;
(b) where the asset is either a non-mobile asset or a dedicated mobile asset used in connection with exploration or exploitation activities in designated areas of the UK continental shelf; or consists of rights to assets to be produced by such activities; or consists of unquoted shares deriving their value from such rights: FA 1973 s 38. At the present time, this extension relates mainly to oil and gas activities in the North Sea.

1.6 Unlike some countries, such as Canada, the UK does not impose a general exit charge to CGT on departing residents. There is an exit charge on UK resident trustees ceasing to be UK resident, or becoming dually resident after 18 March 1991: FA 1991 ss 83, 86, but this does not apply to individuals. For individuals, a tax recapture arises where the individual received a gift from another UK resident within the preceding six years, and capital gains on the gift were rolled over by joint election between donor and beneficiary. On departure, the beneficiary is deemed to realise a capital gain equal to the rolled over gain: FA 1981 s 79. The recapture does not apply where the absence abroad is for three years or less for employment purposes, provided the asset is retained throughout. New UK residents who subsequently dispose of assets acquired when non-resident will be subject to CGT on any gains, which are computed in the normal way by reference to historic cost (or market value at 31 March 1982, where relevant), not market value at the date of becoming resident.

1.7 An individual's domicile does not affect the scope of his liability to income tax or CGT, but it may affect the basis of assessment in certain cases. A UK resident who is domiciled outside the UK is subject to income tax on foreign income such as dividends, interests, rental income and business profits (under Schedule D Case V) on the remittance basis: TA 1988 s 65(5). Tax is charged on the amount of the income actually received in the UK in the tax year (or relevant basis period) rather than on the amount of income arising. The remittance basis also applies to capital gains on the disposal of assets situated outside the UK where the individual is not UK domiciled: CGTA 1979 s 14. Capital losses in such circumstances are not allowable, however: CGTA 1979 s 29(4). The exact scope of the remittance basis, and the definition of a remittance, are explained in subsequent sections of this chapter (see **1.16**).

1.8 For inheritance tax (IHT), the UK gifts and estates tax, residence is not of itself a material factor. Instead, it is the individual's domicile which determines his liability to IHT. Those who are domiciled in the UK are subject to IHT on transfers of any property, on a worldwide basis. Non-domiciled individuals are subject to IHT only on UK situs property. Even here, certain UK government stocks (see Appendix 1) are excluded, provided that the individual is not ordinarily resident in the UK: IHTA 1984 s 6(2). Bank accounts held in the UK by non-UK domiciliaries who are neither resident nor ordinarily resident in the UK are excluded from their estate on death, provided the account is denominated in foreign currency: IHTA 1984 s 157. The latter exemption does not apply to lifetime gifts made out of such accounts. As explained in **3.16**, extended residence in the UK may indirectly affect liability to IHT, since it may result in the individual's being deemed to be UK domiciled: IHTA 1984 s 267.

Territorial limits

1.9 The UK consists of England and Wales, Scotland, and Northern Ireland: Interpretation Act 1978 Sch 1. The Channel Islands and the Isle of Man are not part of the UK. For income tax and CGT, the territorial sea surrounding the UK, up to the three mile limit, is deemed to be part of the UK: TA 1988 s 830(1). In addition, there are provisions bringing within the UK tax net certain income (including employment earnings) and capital gains derived in connection with sea bed exploration and exploitation activities within designated areas of the UK continental shelf: FA 1973 s 38(2)–(5); TA 1988 s 830(3)–(5). A designated area is one designated by Order in Council under s 1(7) of the Continental Shelf Act 1964: TA 1988 s 830(2)(*c*). Designation is in connection with the grant by the Secretary of State of licences for the exploration for and winning of oil and gas. Designated areas are not part of the UK, however, nor are they deemed to be so for UK tax purposes. Presence in a designated area – on an oil rig in the North Sea, for example – does not count as presence in the UK when considering an individual's UK residence status.

Income source and situs of assets

1.10 Whether or not a source of income is situated in the UK depends upon the type of income concerned. Income from various forms of property – land, shares, securities and so on – has its source where the property is situated. Business profits, on the other hand, are treated as arising where the business is managed and controlled: *Colquhoun v Brooks* (1889) 14 App Cas 493, 2 TC 490, HL. For employment income, the legal situs of the service contract is not material, and the 'source' of such income is effectively defined by reference to the place where the duties of the employment are carried out: TA 1988 s 19(1).

1.11 The situs rules for some of the more common types of property are as follows:

Property	*Situs*
Land, interest in land	Where land is physically situated
Shares and securities:	
(a) registered	Where register, or main register, maintained
(b) bearer	Where certificate physically located

Contract debts	Where debtor resides
Bank accounts	Where bank branch situated
Mortgages	Where mortgage registered
Chattels (including currency)	Where physically located

Interest income

1.12   Although UK source interest is in principle taxable in the hands of non-UK residents, there are two important exceptions. The first is that liability to tax on interest from UK bank deposits is not in practice assessed: Extra-statutory concession B13. This concession applies where the individual is not resident throughout the tax year concerned and the interest is not assessable in the name of a UK agent. If the non-resident makes any claim to relief from UK tax in respect of other income which has borne tax, then the tax liability on the interest will be taken into account.

1.13   UK bank deposit interest is subject to tax withholding at source at the basic rate of income tax: TA 1988 s 480A(1). Individual depositors who are not ordinarily resident in the UK are not subject to withholding if they make a written declaration to the bank or other deposit-taker to that effect: TA 1988 s 481(5)(*k*). The declaration must be in a form specified by the Revenue: TA 1988 s 482(2)(*b*). They normally require disclosure of the non-resident's address (or, failing that, an appropriate certificate from the bank), and an undertaking that the bank be notified of any change in residence status: IR Press Release 25 January 1985. Similar rules apply in the case of building society interest receivable by individuals not ordinarily resident in the UK: The Income Tax (Building Societies) (Dividends and Interest) Regulations 1990 SI 1990/2231 Regs 4(1)(a), 11(2), (3).

1.14   Prior to 6 April 1991, bank and building society interest were subject to tax at source at a composite rate which reflected the average rate at which depositors were liable: TA 1988 ss 476, 479. There was a corresponding exemption in the case of non ordinarily resident individuals.

1.15   Individuals not ordinarily resident in the UK are also exempted from UK income tax on interest arising in respect of certain UK government stocks: TA 1988 s 47. A full list is given in Appendix 1. Applications for exemption from withholding are normally filed with the Inspector of Foreign Dividends by the UK bank or stockbroker through whom the stock is acquired.

Remittance basis

1.16   The remittance basis applies chiefly where the individual is resident but not domiciled in the UK, in respect of:

(1) investment income from a non-UK source: TA 1988 s 65(4) and (5);

(2) certain employment income from an employer who is not resident in the UK or the Irish Republic: TA 1988 s 192(2);
(3) pensions from overseas: TA 1988 s 65(4);
(4) trades which are managed and controlled overseas (other than in the Irish Republic): TA 1988 s 65(4).

The remittance basis also applies to:

(5) employment income for the non-UK duties of an individual who is resident but not ordinarily resident in the UK: TA 1988 ss 19(1), 192(1) and (2);
(6) foreign investment income, overseas pensions and overseas trading income of British subjects or Irish citizens not ordinarily resident in the UK: TA 1970 s 65(4).

Income arising in the Republic of Ireland is always taxed in full, however, whether remitted to the UK or not: TA 1988 s 68, save that a deduction of 10% is given in the case of a pension arising in the Republic of Ireland: TA 1988 s 68(5).

1.17 The rules for deciding whether a remittance has been made vary according to the source of income concerned. For foreign securities – such as a mortgage – within Schedule D Case IV, the amount of income assessable is simply the amount received in the UK: TA 1988 s 65(5)(*a*). For other foreign income within Case V, the definition is more detailed and refers to sums received in the UK

(a) from remittances payable in the UK;
(b) from property imported;
(c) from money or value arising from property not imported:
(d) from money or value received in the UK on account of remittances: TA 1988 s 65(5)(*b*).

1.18 For employment income in respect of duties performed outside the UK, the definition differs again and includes earnings paid, used or enjoyed in the UK or brought or transmitted to the UK by whatever means: TA 1988 s 132(5). This definition, which is wider in scope than that under Schedule D, is followed for CGT purposes: CGTA 1979 s 14(1).

1.19 Transfers of cash, or transfers to a UK bank account, will be treated as amounts received in the UK. A draft drawn on a foreign bank can also constitute a remittance even if it is not encashed by the individual but passed on to the payee: *Walsh v Randall* (1940) 23 TC 55, 19 ATC 92. Where the foreign income or capital gain is used to purchase an asset which is then imported into the UK, the importation may constitute a remittance in the case of employment income or capital gains, in view of the wider definitions applicable. For income under Schedule D Case IV or V, there is no remittance until such time as the asset is sold: *Scottish Provident Institution v Farmer* 1912 SC 452, 6 TC 34. On this basis, it is arguable that foreign currency brought to the UK cannot, for the purposes of Schedule D Case IV or V, be regarded as a remittance until such time as it is exchanged for sterling.

1.20 In addition, there are anti-avoidance rules to tax certain indirect remittances of income involving debts: TA 1988 s 65(6)–(9). These provisions catch arrangements whereby money is either borrowed in the UK, or borrowed abroad and imported into the UK, and the debt is then repaid abroad using funds derived from the foreign income or capital gains. The payment for goods and services in the UK with a credit or charge card appears to be regarded by the Inland Revenue as falling within these provisions if the cardholder's account was settled outside the UK with funds representing foreign source income. However, it is arguable that, in law, the card user incurs a debt to the card provider, not to the UK supplier of goods or services. Thus, where the card provider is resident outside the UK, there is no UK debt, nor is any advance made outside the UK imported into the UK. In addition, there is a remittance if the overseas debt is repaid with such funds before the money borrowed is brought into the UK, but only if the individual concerned is ordinarily resident in the UK: TA 1988 s 65(7).

1.21 The anti-avoidance rules also counter back-to-back arrangements whereby funds derived from the foreign income or gains are available to repay money borrowed and brought into the UK, even though no repayment is in fact effected while the individual is UK resident: TA 1988 s 65(8). Indirect borrowing through corporate vehicles has also been treated as a remittance: *Harmel v Wright* [1974] 1 All ER 945, [1974] STC 88. In that case, funds representing overseas income were subscribed for shares in an offshore company controlled by the taxpayer. The funds were in turn lent by that company to another offshore company not controlled by him, which lent him the funds in the UK. The court decided that the overseas income could be traced through and therefore constituted a remittance. It is debatable whether this robust approach would be followed in all cases where funds were channelled through overseas companies.

1.22 Notwithstanding the various rules outlined, there remain a number of methods of avoiding UK tax on the remittance of funds to the UK by non-domiciled individuals. The most obvious is to remit funds only out of capital held abroad. Difficulties arise in the case of remittances out of mixed funds deriving partly from income, partly from capital and/or capital gains. The Revenue usually take the approach that partial remittances out of mixed funds should be considered primarily as income, then capital gain (if any), then capital. The alternative view often adopted by the taxpayer is that such remittances should be allocated rateably between the various constituent elements of the fund. The latter approach is thought to have found favour with the Special Commissioners, although the point has not been tested in the courts. Wherever possible, the problem should be avoided by segregating income, capital and mixed capital/capital gains into separate bank accounts overseas, so that remittances may clearly be identified. The mitigation of income tax on foreign source income of non-UK domiciled individuals is further considered in **8.18–8.25**.

1.23 Where funds are needed to meet personal expenditure, it may still be possible to avoid UK tax by using the income funds to pay such expenses outside the UK, or to purchase assets for importation into the UK. In the latter case, tax may be avoided if the asset is used in the UK but re-exported prior to sale, although the position is doubtful if the asset has been purchased with foreign employment income or capital gains (see **1.19**). If the asset is of a wasting nature such as clothing or household appliances which are unlikely to have a material resale value any potential liability on importation can be minimised. Funds may alternatively be used to make gifts to members of the family, which they then import into the UK: *Carter v Sharon* [1936] 1 All ER 720, 20 TC 229. Such arrangements are effective only if there is a bona fide gift, preferably evidenced in writing, and the money is not simply returned to the donor after being remitted to the UK. It is also possible to avoid UK tax on foreign income (but not capital gains) if the income is not remitted to the UK until after the end of the tax year in which the source ceased to exist – for example, if a bank account has been closed. This device is no longer effective in relation to employments, since receipts in the UK of earnings are still taxable even though the employment has ceased in an earlier tax year: TA 1988 s 202A.

Personal allowances

1.24 Personal allowances are available generally to individuals resident in the UK: TA 1988 s 256. However, certain non-residents may also claim allowances: TA 1988 s 278. Those entitled to claim are:

(a) Commonwealth citizens;
(b) Irish citizens;
(c) present or past civil servants, and widows or widowers of former civil servants;
(d) missionaries;
(e) public servants of Crown Protectorates;
(f) residents of the Channel Islands or the Isle of Man;
(g) former UK residents who are abroad for the sake of their health or that of a member of their family resident with them;
(h) foreign residents entitled to claim under the terms of a double taxation agreement.

1.25 For 1989/90 and earlier years, personal allowances granted to non-residents could not reduce their UK income tax liability below a proportion of the notional liability calculated on the basis that all their income worldwide was subject to tax on the arising basis: *Mackillop v IRC* [1943] 2 All ER 215, 25 TC 280, CA. In computing the notional tax, no credit was given for any foreign tax actually suffered on the income: *IRC v Watts* (1958) 38 TC 146, [1958] TR 257. The proportion was the ratio between UK taxable income and worldwide income. In other words, the allowances could not reduce the tax rate on UK income below the notional average rate on world income. Despite the rules regarding aggregation of the income of married couples, the income of a non-resident spouse was not included in world income: *IRC v Addison* [1984] 1 WLR 1264, [1984] STC 540. Income from exempt gilt-edged stock (see **1.15**) was included in worldwide income for this purpose but excluded from UK taxable income as was any UK source income exempted from tax under the terms of a double taxation agreement.

EXAMPLE

1.26 AB who is married is not resident in the UK but is entitled to claim proportionate personal allowances. For 1989/90, details of his income are as follows:

	UK	*Worldwide*
UK rental income (net)	£ 5,000	£ 5,000
UK exempt gilts interest		4,000
Employment in Canada		6,000
UK directorships	15,000	15,000
	20,000	30,000
Personal allowance	4,375	4,375
Taxable income	£15,625	£25,625
UK income tax	£ 3,906.25	£ 7,145.00

Minimum tax if allowances claimed: $\frac{20,000}{30,000} \times £7,145.00 = £4,763.33$

UK income tax if no allowances claimed: 5,000.00

Relief due (in terms of tax) if allowances claimed: £ 236.67

1.27 If the non-resident was entitled under the terms of a double tax agreement to a reduced rate of UK tax on UK dividends, interest or royalties, the income concerned was included in worldwide income but excluded from UK income in the relevant fraction. Notional UK tax on world income was calculated without reference to any double taxation relief due. As a result, the personal allowances claim had no effect upon the rate of tax charged on the income in question. UK dividend income for this purpose included any tax credit refunded under the terms of the tax treaty concerned: IR20 para 61. The mechanism of the refund is explained at **1.44** below. Non-resident individuals whose sole UK source of income consist of treaty relieved dividends, interest or royalties did not normally derive any benefit from a personal allowances claim unless the notional rate of tax on worldwide income was lower than the treaty rate for the income in question.

EXAMPLE

1.28 JK has income sources for 1989/90 as follows:

	UK	*Worldwide*
UK dividends (net)	£ 3,600	£ 3,600
UK employment income	20,000	20,000

He is a Swiss resident and claims personal allowances under article 23 of the UK/Switzerland double taxation treaty. He is unmarried. Under article 10 of the double taxation treaty JK is entitled to a refund of tax credit on the dividends, subject to a withholding tax of 15%.

UK income		£20,000
Worldwide income:		
UK dividends	£ 3,600	
Tax credit (1/3)	1,200	£ 4,800
UK earnings		20,000
		24,800
Personal allowance		2,785
		£22,015

Income tax on £22,015	£ 5,701.00
Minimum UK tax: $\dfrac{20,000}{24,800} \times £5,701.00$	£ 4,597.58
Income tax on £20,000 without allowances	£ 5,000.00
Allowances given, in terms of tax	£ 402.42

UK tax on the dividends is £720 (15% of £4,800) and is unaffected by the claim.

Income deductions

1.29 Residence status does not in itself have any effect upon the deductions that are allowable in computing income from any particular source. The rules for computing income are the same whether the individual is resident or non-resident. However, non-residence may have both direct and indirect effects upon the deductions to be made in computing total income. Such deductions are not set off against particular sources of income but are deducted from aggregate income from all sources.

1.30 One of the main such deductions is interest on a loan to acquire or to improve the individual's main residence, assuming that it is in the UK: TA 1988 ss 354(1), 355(1)(*a*). A non-resident's main home may well not be in the UK, hence the deduction will not be available. Where it is available, relief will be given only for interest on a loan of up to £30,000; where the loan exceeds that limit, the allowable interest is reduced rateably: TA 1988 s 357. In many cases, tax relief is given at the basic rate of income tax by deduction at source when the interest is paid (the MIRAS scheme): TA 1988 s 369. The mere fact that an individual is non-resident does not preclude the payment of interest within MIRAS.

1.31 In order to qualify for tax relief, interest paid on home loans must be paid or payable in the UK in respect of non-overdraft advances from UK banks, from UK branches of foreign banks, or must otherwise constitute UK source taxable income in the hands of the lender: TA 1988 s 353(1) and (2). Interest relief is not available in respect of non-UK borrowings, and this may in practice limit the flexibility on non-residents in arranging their borrowings. The requirement that loans be taken in the UK also applies to relief for interest where a property is commercially let: TA 1988 s 355(1)(*b*). However, such interest would not in any event be within MIRAS, and any tax relief is given when the income is assessed.

Life assurance premiums

1.32 Tax relief on life assurance premiums is no longer available on new policies. Relief at 12.5% continues to be available for qualifying policies issued on or before 13 March 1984. Relief is not generally available to non-residents: TA 1988 s 266(5)(*a*). However, members of the armed forces, their wives, women serving in the WRNS, WRAC or WAAF and their husbands continue to be entitled to relief by deduction from premiums, even if they are not UK resident: TA 1988 s 266(9). Non-residents claiming personal allowances under TA 1988 s 278 are also entitled to relief for premiums, which is given by set off in the claim: TA 1988 s 266(8). If a UK resident individual becomes non-resident, relief on premiums is withdrawn and they must thereafter be paid gross unless and until they resume residence in the UK. Loss of UK resident status may also have an effect upon the deduction of pension plan contributions (see **7.14**).

Married couples

1.33 From 1990/91 onwards, a married woman is a taxpayer in her own right and is assessable on her income and capital gains in the normal way. Prior to 1990/91, the income of a married woman living with her husband was deemed to be his income: TA 1988 s 279. This rule did not apply where either the wife or the husband was non-UK resident for the tax year, whilst the other remained resident throughout, or they were both resident but one was absent from the UK throughout the year: TA 1988 s 282 (as originally enacted). In that case, they were treated as if they were permanently separated for the year, and were hence taxed as single individuals. This treatment could not increase their overall tax liability.

1.34 For capital gains tax, transfers of assets between a husband and wife living together are deemed to be on a no gain, no loss basis: CGTA 1979 s 44. This is so whether or not they are both UK resident, and, prior to 1990/91, the rule treating them as separated could not create a liability in these circumstances: *Gubay v Kington* [1984] 1 All ER 513, [1984] STC 99, HL. It is therefore possible for assets to be sold free of CGT by first transferring them to a non-resident spouse, who is not subject to CGT. There is a risk that the intermediate transfer would be ignored for tax purposes if it were made purely to avoid CGT: *Furniss v Dawson* [1984] AC 474, [1984] STC 153, HL.

1.35 Transfers of property between spouses who are both UK domiciled or both domiciled outside the UK are free of inheritance tax: IHTA 1984 s 18(1). If one of them is domiciled and the other not, transfers to the non-domiciled spouse are exempt only up to a cumulative limit of £55,000 within the 7 year period for potentially exempt transfers (see IHTA 1984 s 3A): IHTA 1984 s 18(2).

Tax withholding

1.36 Withholding of tax at source on certain classes of income applies regardless of the residence status of the recipient. The main example is interest paid by UK resident companies and local authorities: TA 1988 s 349. By contrast, UK bank interest, although normally subject to withholding at source, may be paid gross to non-residents (see **1.13**).

1.37 In certain cases, withholding tax is applied only where the recipient is non-resident. Rental income from UK real estate is subject to withholding at the basic rate of income tax (25% for 1991/92) where paid directly to an individual whose usual place of abode is outside the UK: TA 1988 s 43. The withholding applies to the gross rental. It is not a final tax but is credited against the income tax liability, if any, on the net rental, any excess being repayable. The expression 'usual place of abode' is not defined for this purpose, but is defined elsewhere as the country where a person normally lives: TA 1988 s 195(9) (see **8.32**).

1.38 The withholding on rental income may normally be avoided if the rent is paid to a UK agent, in whose name any income tax is assessed: TMA 1970 s 78. Estate agents managing a property are often prepared to accept this responsibility, subject to an acceptable indemnity from the non-resident in addition to payment of normal professional fees. However, there is evidence that the Revenue are challenging arrangements where the agent does no more than receive the rent, on the grounds that he is acting as a mere nominee.

1.39 Copyright royalties are also subject to withholding at the basic rate of income tax where the copyright owner's usual place of abode is outside the UK: TA 1988 s 536. The withholding does not apply to film royalties, nor to royalties in respect of distribution of copyright items outside the UK. The gross amount of any royalty is normally subject to withholding, but any fee payable to a UK collecting agent is deductible.

1.40 Payments made to non-resident entertainers and sportsmen are subject to withholding at the basic rate of income tax where the payment is in connection with a defined UK activity: TA 1988 s 555. The requirement to account for income tax also applies to transfer of property other than cash, and to loans. The UK activity is treated as a trade or profession carried on in the UK, even if the entertainer etc is an employee: TA 1988 s 556. Relevant activities are widely defined to include any activity as an entertainer in connection with a commercial event, or an appearance to promote such an event, as well as participation in sound recordings, films, videos or TV transmissions: Income Tax (Entertainers and Sportsmen) Regulations 1987 SI 1987/530 reg 6. Payments etc for endorsement, sponsorship and advertising are caught, as well as fees for performances and appearances. Payments to non-resident controlled companies, or non-resident trusts where the entertainer is a settlor, are also caught: reg 7. The person making the payment is responsible for withholding and accounting for income tax.

1.41 A reduced rate of withholding may be authorised by the Revenue on prior application, where it can be shown that the withholding would otherwise be in excess of the correct tax liability eg because of expenses, or because a double taxation treaty grants immunity. The Revenue normally expect such an application to include:

(a) the date of arrival and departure from the UK;
(b) a projection of income, details of expenses to be incurred, and other relevant background information eg analysis of commissions paid, air fares and hotel costs;
(c) copies of the principal contacts relating to the appearances;
(d) the venues and dates of the appearances.

Applications are made to the Inland Revenue Foreign Entertainers Unit (see Appendix 3), who administer the foreign entertainers and sportsmen withholding tax arrangements.

Double taxation agreements

1.42 In addition to the UK statutory provisions which determine the treatment of various sources of income, there are double taxation agreements between the UK and other countries which may modify the position. The UK has entered into more than 80 comprehensive tax treaties, with both developed and less developed nations.

1.43 Individuals who are resident in the UK may claim relief from tax in another country under the terms of an applicable tax treaty between that country and the UK. Non-UK residents cannot normally claim under UK tax treaties, except insofar as they can claim relief from UK tax as a resident of the other country: TA 1988 s 794. Although the precise scope varies from treaty to treaty, the following main reliefs are generally found:

(a) business income: exemption where the individual is not present in the country for more than 183 days and has no fixed base;
(b) employment income: exemption where the individual is not present in the country for more than 183 days, the employer is not resident in that country, and the remuneration is not charged to a branch of the employer in that country;
(c) interest and royalties: reduction of withholding tax rate, or complete exemption, in the country where the income arises;
(d) dividends: reduction of withholding tax rate, as in (c), and – in the case of UK dividends – entitlement to refund of the tax credit;
(e) personal allowances: entitlement to claim in the same way as a non-resident national of the country concerned (see **1.24**).

Special provisions commonly apply to company directors, artistes and athletes, visiting teachers, pensioners and students. In many treaties, there is also an 'other income' article which restricts taxation of miscellaneous income, not expressly referred to elsewhere in the treaty, to the country of residence.

1.44 Where refund of tax credit is granted under a UK tax treaty in respect of UK dividends, a non-resident individual is generally subject to a withholding tax of 15% on the aggregate of the dividend and the tax credit. This means that, with the basic rate of income tax at 25%, the net refund will be 2/15 of the dividend:

Dividend received		75
Tax credit (1/3)	25	
Tax (15% × 100)	(15)	10
Total receipt		85

1.45 There are exceptions to the general rule that only UK residents may claim double taxation relief in the UK: TA 1988 s 794(2).

(a) Residents of the Isle of Man or the Channel Islands may claim relief for tax in those territories against UK tax on the same income.
(b) Residents of a treaty country may claim relief against UK tax for tax charged there on employment income, where the duties are performed wholly or mainly in that country. Thus, non-UK residents charged under Schedule E Case II on earnings for UK duties may credit tax charged in their home country, on a rateable basis.

Double taxation relief

1.46 In the UK, double taxation relief for foreign tax is given by way of credit against the UK tax on the same source of income or capital gains (see **4.35–4.42**). Excess credit cannot be carried forward or back, or be used against UK tax on another income source. It is possible to treat foreign tax as a deduction from UK income: TA 1970 s 811. Where credit would otherwise be due, an election may be made not to allow credit: TA 1988 s 805. Such an election must cover the whole of the foreign tax, not merely the excess, and is normally of benefit only where the source produces a loss for UK tax purposes. For non-residents claiming double taxation relief for UK tax, the manner in which relief is given depends upon the domestic tax code of the country concerned, as modified by any applicable treaty. Credit may be available (in the US, for example) or instead the income concerned may be exempted from local tax (as in some European countries).

2 Residence

2.1 As noted in the preceding summary of the UK personal tax system, the concept of residence is central to the determination of liability to income tax and capital gains tax. Individuals who are resident in the UK are subject to income tax on worldwide income and to capital gains tax on all their assets, wherever situated. Those who are not resident are subject to income tax only on UK sources of income, and to capital gains tax in respect only of certain business assets situated in the UK. An individual's residence status is also, in many cases, an important factor as regards entitlement to tax reliefs, such as personal allowances. For expatriates another important implication of tax residence is the application of double taxation agreements. Only UK residents can claim relief from foreign tax under tax treaties entered into by the UK (see **1.43**).

The meaning of 'residence'

2.2 Despite its importance, the meaning of residence is not comprehensively defined in the tax statutes. The criteria for determining residence are instead derived largely from a long line of judgments handed down by the courts, although many of the leading cases are now of some antiquity. In addition, there are a number of statutory rules which extend or modify the concept of residence: TA 1988 ss 334–336. Based upon the judgments and legislation, the Revenue have developed a practical set of rules, which are set out in their booklet IR20 'Residents and non-residents: Liability to tax in the United Kingdom'. These practical rules have no statutory force. Although they are not unchallengeable, the rules are in general beneficial to the taxpayer and perhaps for that reason are usually accepted. There are, doubtless, points of principle still to be established, but decided cases on questions of residence seem to have become a rarity, with *Reed v Clark* (see **2.3**) and *R v IRC, ex p Fulford-Dobson* (see **6.45**) being the only judgments on questions of individual residence in the space of over 15 years.

Physical presence

2.3 Residence, for UK tax purposes, is not the same as nationality or legal domicile, nor is it dependent upon them in any way. In essence, residence is concerned with physical presence in the UK at some time during the tax year. If an individual does not set foot in the UK at any time in the tax year it is probable that he will not be UK resident for that year (see IR20 para 9).

There is an element of doubt, however, in certain circumstances. Commonwealth (and Irish) citizens who have been ordinarily resident in the UK but who have left the UK for the purpose of 'occasional' residence abroad are to continue to be charged to income tax as UK residents: TA 1988 s 334. The Revenue have invoked this provision in cases where individuals have left the UK for a year with the intention of avoiding an income tax or capital gains tax charge in that year. In a case involving a pop musician who became non-resident for one complete tax year to avoid UK income tax, the Revenue were unsuccessful in their contention that residence continued for tax purposes: *Reed v Clark* [1986] Ch 1, [1985] STC 323. It was held that the period of residence abroad was a sufficiently material change in the taxpayer's pattern of life to be distinguishable from mere 'occasional' residence abroad.

2.4 Where an individual is present in the UK at some time in the tax year, it is a question of fact and degree whether he is resident for that year: *IRC v Lysaght* [1928] AC 234, 13 TC 511, HL. However, the individual's intentions are not a decisive consideration nor is it relevant that the individual's presence may not be entirely voluntary: *Lord Inchiquin v IRC* (1948) 31 TC 125 [1948] TR 343. What is more important is an element of permanence in the individual's UK presence, in the sense that the UK becomes, for a time at least, the individual's home. It is not necessary that there should be a permanent abode available to the individual in the UK, and even those living in hotels have been held to be resident in the UK: *Reid v IRC* 1926 SC 589, 10 TC 673; *Levene v IRC* [1928] AC 217, 13 TC 486, HL. It is possible for an individual to be resident in the UK even if he has a permanent home elsewhere.

The 183-day rule

2.5 If an individual has no permanent abode available to him in the UK, he will not be treated as UK resident unless his visits to the UK are either extended, or repeated from year to year, or both. It is made clear by the statute that an individual will be taxed as a resident if he spends, in aggregate, six months or more in the UK: TA 1988 s 336. The Revenue regard this rule as admitting of no exceptions (IR20 para 8) and it could therefore operate harshly where continued presence in the UK is outside the individual's control – for example, because of illness. Six months, in strictness, means six calendar months, counting hours as well as days: *Wilkie v IRC* [1952] Ch 153, 32 TC 495. In practice, six months is taken as equivalent to 183 days, and days of arrival and departure are not normally counted. The concession set out in SP2/91 (see **2.6**) does *not* apply to the 183-day rule.

Repeated visits

2.6 Where there are repeated visits to the UK, an individual is treated as becoming resident once his visits average three months a year over four consecutive years (IR20 para 21). However, provided that visits to the UK are for a temporary purpose only and there is no intention of establishing residence, days spent in the UK as a result of exceptional circumstances beyond the individual's control are left out of account: Statement of Practice SP2/91. The Statement of Practice cites illness as an example of a relevant circumstance, but the practice would also apply where the individual returned to the UK from an overseas assignment as a result of war or civil unrest in a foreign country, such as the Gulf War. Residence can begin at the outset if there is then a clear intention to make such repeated visits to the UK. The three month average has no statutory basis.

Available accommodation

2.7 An individual who spends less than 183 days in the UK in the tax year may or may not be UK resident, depending upon the circumstances. He will not be taxed as a resident if he is in the UK for a temporary purpose only: TA 1988 s 336, but this exemption really does little more than to restate the general guideline laid down by the courts. Unquestionably, the single most important factor in this situation is whether the individual has a place of abode in the UK. In the view of the Revenue, a visitor who has accommodation available in the UK is resident for any tax year in which he sets foot in the UK (IR20 para 21). This view is founded upon a series of judgments in which foreigners taking accommodation in the UK were held to be resident here even though their permanent home was abroad and only a relatively short period was spent in the UK (for example, *IRC v Cadwalader* 1904 7 F (Ct of Sess) 146, 5 TC 101). Nevertheless, there are circumstances in which the Revenue view could conceivably be challenged; for example, where a single visit was made to the UK in the tax year, without actually residing in the accommodation concerned.

2.8 One important aspect of the rule regarding available accommodation is that the individual need not have any legal title to or interest in the accommodation (IR20 para 28). Property owned by an employer but held available for the employee's use can also result in the individual becoming UK resident: *Loewenstein v de Salis* (1926) 10 TC 424. Similarly, rooms kept ready for an individual in the home of a relative or friend could constitute available accommodation, depending upon the circumstances. The existence or absence of a legal right to occupy or use accommodation is not conclusive. Nevertheless, available accommodation is ignored if rented for a temporary stay in the UK and the period of renting is less than two years for furnished accommodation, or one year for unfurnished (IR20 para 28).

Employment abroad

2.9 In addition to the Revenue practice just referred to, there is a statutory disregard of available accommodation in circumstances where the individual works full-time in an employment, the duties of which are carried on wholly outside the UK: TA 1988 s 335. This disregard also applies where the individual carries on a trade or profession wholly outside the UK. In the case of employments only, duties performed in the UK are treated as performed abroad if they are merely incidental to the performance of other duties actually carried out abroad: TA 1988 s 335(3).

'Incidental' duties

2.10   There is no statutory definition of 'incidental to' although it is clear that the Revenue would expect incidental duties to be minimal, such as reporting back to the UK head office, attending conferences in the UK and so on. Visits to the UK of up to three months purely for training purposes are regarded as incidental to overseas duties if no productive work is done while in the UK (IR20 para 39). Executive directors of a UK company who work wholly abroad are unlikely to be able to show that attending UK board meetings is incidental to the performance of the executive duties elsewhere. The nature of the UK duties, and their relationship to the other duties performed abroad, rather than merely the relative time devoted to them, are the governing factors: *Robson v Dixon* [1972] 3 All ER 671, 48 TC 527. In that particular case, an airline pilot made a small number of take-offs and landings in the UK during the tax year, and a much larger number outside the UK. However, the UK duties were held not to be incidental to the duties performed abroad. It appears that the Revenue would disregard a single take-off and landing, on *de minimis* grounds: Statement of Practice SP/A10. If the UK duties are performed for a period of more than three months in any year, then, regardless of what they involve, the Revenue do not regard them as incidental to the performance of other duties outside the UK (IR20 para 38).

Ordinary residence

2.11   Ordinary residence is a UK tax concept in addition to that of residence which affects the basis of assessment of income tax in some circumstances, and can determine liability to capital gains tax. It is also important in relation to the application of certain anti-avoidance provisions which counter the transfer of income to non-residents: TA 1988 ss 739 and 740. Like residence, ordinary residence is not formally defined in the tax legislation and reference must be made to the decided cases. Ordinary residence is not identical with residence but implies an habitual or customary residence from one tax year to another, as contrasted with occasional or casual residence: *IRC v Lysaght* [1928] AC 234, 13 TC 511, HL. Ordinary residence is also a matter of fact and degree and it is not material whether the individual stays in the UK from personal choice: *Miesegaes v IRC* (1957) 37 TC 493, [1957] TR 231, CA. Moreover, ordinary residence in the UK is not inconsistent with having a permanent home abroad, and need not be associated with lengthy periods spent in the UK.

2.12   The Revenue adopt a number of rules of thumb in determining ordinary residence. An individual treated as UK resident by virtue of repeated visits averaging three months or more over a four-year period will also be treated as ordinarily resident: IR20 para 21 (see **2.6**). Similarly, an individual who is resident for other reasons, such as having available accommodation in the UK, will also be treated as ordinarily resident if he visits the UK, or intends to do so, each year during a period of four or more consecutive years.

Residence changes

2.13   By implication, residence and ordinary residence are tax attributes which an individual possesses for the whole of a given tax year, even though he might be physically present in the UK for one part of the year, and absent for another. Income tax, and capital gains tax, are charged for a given tax year and the charging provisions do not contemplate the possibility that a tax year might need to be split into two or more parts for each of which the individual had a different residence status. This is the view taken explicitly by the Revenue (IR20 para 11). For example, an individual present in the UK for 184 days continuously in the tax year, but absent for the whole of the rest of it, would be treated as resident for the whole year, not just for the period spent in the UK. In practice, however, the Revenue do split the tax year in circumstances in which individuals become or cease to be 'permanent' residents of the UK, or leave the UK to take up a full-time employment contract outside the UK, part way through the year.

2.14   An individual may be regarded as ceasing to be resident and ordinarily resident in the UK from the day following departure for permanent residence abroad. Permanent residence abroad is not defined but would, for example, include circumstances where the UK home was sold and a new home acquired elsewhere (IR20 para 16). As indicated earlier, permanence in the tax context is a relative matter, and it would not be necessary to demonstrate that there was an intention never to return to the UK. Where an individual convinces the Revenue that he has departed to live abroad permanently, the normal rules relating to visits back to the UK nevertheless still apply, so that the individual will be resident for any year in which he spends 183 days or more in the UK. Equally, he will not lose his UK resident and ordinarily resident status if his visits back to the UK average three months or more per tax year. If living accommodation continues to be available in the UK, the individual may be resident for any tax year in which he sets foot in the UK.

2.15   The Revenue will normally give a provisional non-resident ruling effective from the date following departure if the individual can demonstrate that he has relinquished UK resident status. Evidence of such a change in residence status would include disposal of the individual's private residence in the UK and acquisition of a new home abroad. The ruling is confirmed after at least one complete tax year has been spend abroad provided that visits to the UK average less than three months each tax year. If evidence of non-residence is not available, the individual will not be given a non-resident ruling until at least three years have elapsed. During that period, he will continue to be taxed, provisionally, as a UK resident (IR 20 para 17).

Overseas employments

2.16   A UK resident going abroad to work may find it less onerous than the non-employed emigré to prove non-resident status. In particular, retaining a home in the UK need not prejudice the expatriate employee's tax position. Provided that the duties of the employment are performed wholly outside the UK, and the period of absence is to span at least one complete tax year, the individual will normally be regarded as provisionally not resident and not ordinarily resident from the date following departure (IR20 para 18). The tax implications are discussed in chapter 7. The normal restrictions on visits back to the UK apply (see **2.14**). Work-related visits to the UK need not prejudice the individual's status since duties can be performed in the UK provided they are purely incidental to the performance of the employee's duties abroad. This concessional treatment does not apply to self-employed individuals eg a person moving abroad to become a partner in an overseas firm.

Coming to the UK

2.17 Analogous rules are applied by the Revenue where individuals from abroad visit the UK for an extended period. In general, visits intended to be for a period of three years or more result in acquisition of UK resident and ordinarily resident status from the date of arrival (not from the beginning of the tax year in which the individual arrives). If, at the time he arrives, the immigrant has no definite intention as to residence, he is treated as resident but not ordinarily resident on arrival. Once the individual has been resident continuously for three years following arrival in the UK, he is treated as ordinarily resident from the beginning of the tax year in which the third anniversary falls. If, before that, he decides to remain in the UK on a permanent basis, then he would be ordinarily resident from the beginning of the tax year in which that decision is taken (IR20 para 26). Alternatively, the availability of accommodation in the UK in the tax year of arrival can be taken as indicating that the individual has become ordinarily resident, provided that the accommodation is occupied on a basis implying a stay of three years or more.

2.18 Visitors to the UK for study or education are treated as resident and ordinarily resident from the date of arrival if the stay is expected to last for more than four years. Otherwise, the individual is not treated as becoming ordinarily resident until the beginning of the fifth year.

2.19 For visits lasting less than three years, residence status will normally be determined separately for each tax year involved. However, expatriate employees coming to the UK to work for two years or more are treated as resident from the date of arrival (IR20 para 25). This could be of benefit to the expatriate – for example, in enabling personal allowances to be claimed for the year of arrival.

Married women

2.20 A married woman's residence status is determined on the basis of her own circumstances and does not necessarily coincide with that of her husband. Prior to 1990/91, where one of them was UK resident and the other not, their income was taxed as if they were single persons, if this was advantageous to them: TA 1988 s 282 (as originally enacted). This treatment would be of benefit, for example, where the wife was non-resident but had investment income arising in the UK.

Dual residence

2.21 It is possible for UK resident individuals to be resident in one or more other countries at the same time. This may occur where the other country's criterion of residence is different from that in the UK. For example, an individual might spend most of the year living in a particular country abroad, whilst returning regularly to a home in the UK. Alternatively, where the other country's tax year did not coincide with the UK tax year, the individual might become resident there before ceasing to be UK resident. In these circumstances, both countries will normally have the right to tax the individual's income, although, at worst, relief for foreign tax suffered will be available unilaterally in the UK.

Double taxation treaties

2.22 If there is a double taxation treaty between the UK and the other country, some further relief may normally be obtained from double taxation of income and capital gains. Most treaties now contain 'tie-breaker' rules under which a dually resident individual's residence status must be resolved for the purpose of applying the treaty. It is essential to do this in order to establish which country is to relinquish or limit its taxation rights over particular sources of income, and which is to give relief for any residual double taxation suffered. The determination of residence for this purpose has no effect on the individual's residence status within each country's domestic tax code. This is an important consideration in cases where relief is afforded by the tax treaty only for sources of income in one or other of the two countries concerned, so that income arising in a third country could be taxed in both countries of residence. However, personal allowances should be available in both countries on the basis that the individual is resident.

2.23 The standard structure of the 'tie-breaker' provision in most modern treaties is that a number of tests are applied in sequence. If a given test does not resolve the individual's residence status, the next test in the sequence is applied, and so on. As a last resort, the position is to be determined by mutual agreement between the two tax authorities. This remedy is generally better avoided; it can be a lengthy procedure and the individual may not have any right of appeal. The text of the OECD model treaty article, which is adopted in most modern UK conventions, is reproduced at Appendix 2.

Claims and appeals

2.24 Claims regarding residence and ordinary residence are made to the Board of Inland Revenue within six years of the end of the tax year to which they relate. In practice, claims are filed with the local Inspector of Taxes and referred by him to Claims Branch, Foreign Division (see Appendix 3 for the address and telephone number). Where the Revenue decision on a residence claim is disputed, the taxpayer may appeal to the Special Commissioners within three months of receiving written notice of the decision: TMA 1970 s 42(3), Sch 2. The Special Commissioners are an appellate tribunal appointed by the Lord Chancellor and appointees are solicitors or barristers of at least 10 years standing: TMA 1970 s 4. They normally meet in London to hear appeals, although appeals are also heard on circuit in certain centres outside London.

2.25 Appeals may be made from a decision of the Special Commissioners to the High Court, but only on a question of law. The Special Commissioners state a case for consideration by the courts, which sets out the facts as found by the Commissioners and the contentions advanced by each party, together with the Commissioners' decision. No new evidence can be brought forward on an appeal to the Courts. The Special Commissioners' decision can be overturned only if it is wrong in law or if, on the facts found, it is a decision that no reasonable body of Commissioners, properly instructed as to the law, could have reached: *Edwards v Bairstow and Harrison* [1955] 3 All ER 48, 36 TC 207, HL. On questions of residence, which are essentially matters of fact, the presentation of evidence before the Commissioners is therefore of the utmost importance and it is likely to be relatively difficult for an individual to succeed in the courts on a case where the Special Commissioners have given an adverse decision on his residence status. Equally, a decision by the Commissioners which is favourable to the taxpayer can only with difficulty be overturned on appeal by the Revenue.

3 Domicile

3.1 Residence is an important tax concept in the UK because it determines the territorial scope of UK income tax, non-residents being taxed only on UK sources of income. Ordinary residence, essentially an extension of residence, has implications for tax liability in the case of employment income and capital gains. A further factor which may affect an individual's UK tax position is domicile. For income tax and capital gains tax, domicile has no effect upon the territorial scope of the tax, but determines the basis of assessment where the income or gains arise abroad. Individuals domiciled outside the UK are taxed only on remittances to the UK of foreign sources of income, or of gains on the disposal of assets situated outside the UK: TA 1988 s 65(4), (5); CGTA 1979 s 14(1). However, for inheritance tax, domicile does determine the territorial scope in that, for those domiciled outside the UK, only property situated in the UK is within the scope of IHT: IHTA 1984 s 6(1).

3.2 Domicile therefore has considerable practical significance for those coming from abroad to visit or live in the UK – and also for those who leave the UK to make a new home in another country. Unlike residence and ordinary residence, however, domicile has ramifications beyond the sphere of taxation. It is, indeed, central in the field of private international law, and determines which system of law is to govern personal transactions such as succession; marriage and divorce; legitimacy; and questions of legal capacity. Many other countries have adopted nationality as the governing factor in determining which system of law is to be the individual's personal law, but domicile is distinct from nationality. It is also different from residence and ordinary residence as defined for UK tax purposes, although residence is relevant in determining domicile.

Meaning of domicile

3.3 There is no statutory definition of domicile, but its meaning has been established by decisions of the courts over the years. Briefly stated, an individual's domicile is the place – in the sense of a territory having its own system of law – which is to be regarded as his home. Domicile has also been described as the individual's 'centre of gravity': *Re Flynn, Flynn v Flynn* [1968] 1 WLR 103 at 119. It is generally accepted that domicile need not be an independent state but can be a political subdivision, provided it has an independent system of law, such as Scotland or one of the individual states of the USA. However, the position is not always clear cut, since such subdivisions of a state will also be subject to the law of the larger territory of which they form a part. This question may be relevant in the tax context, as explained below (see **3.10**).

Domicile of origin

3.4 It is a fundamental principle that every individual must at all times have a domicile: *Udny v Udny* (1869) LR 1 Sc & Div 441, 7 Macq 89, HL. Those who are not of full age or who otherwise are under some legal incapacity cannot establish an independent domicile and consequently legal principles have been developed to attribute a domicile to such individuals. Domicile of origin is a domicile automatically acquired by all individuals at birth and is determined solely on the basis of parentage, without reference to the place of birth. The domicile of a legitimate child born during its father's lifetime is its father's domicile at its date of birth. Illegitimate children, or legitimate children born after the death of their father, take the domicile of the mother at the date of birth. However, there can sometimes be difficulties in determining the domicile of children whose parents have different domiciles, since legitimacy may itself depend upon the child's domicile. Subsequent legitimation of illegitimate children does not normally change their domicile of origin. In general, domicile of origin cannot be changed by any subsequent event or act by the individual, although their current domicile may change, as explained below. It is important to note that an individual need never have set foot in the territory which is his domicile of origin.

Domicile of dependency

3.5 An individual's domicile of origin continues indefinitely to be his domicile unless and until he acquires a new domicile. There are two ways in which this may happen. First, individuals who are not of full age will acquire a new domicile if there is a change in the domicile of the parent, from whom they derive their domicile of origin. The child's domicile is termed domicile of dependence. This is to oversimplify matters somewhat, and the position is more complex where one or both of the parents die before the child is of full age, or they become separated or divorced. The domicile of adopted children is related to their adoptive rather than their natural parents, although adoption does not normally have any effect upon domicile of origin.

Domicile of choice

3.6 The second circumstance in which domicile can change is where an individual of full age, and not otherwise legally incapacitated, voluntarily adopts a new domicile. In England, an individual is capable of having an independent domicile on attaining the age of 16: Domicile and Matrimonial Proceedings Act 1973 s 3(1). The relevant age in Scotland is 14 for boys, 12 for girls. A domicile acquired voluntarily is referred to as a domicile of choice. For a domicile of choice to be effective, two essential requirements must be met. First, the individual must take up residence in the country concerned. Residence for this purpose need not be extended, nor does it involve the possession of a fixed place of abode. The second requirement is that there must be an intention to remain indefinitely, or without time limit, in the adopted country or state: *Udny v Udny* (1869) LR 1 Sc & Div 441, 7 Macq 89, HL. Extended residence without the necessary intention will not result in a change of domicile. Because a domicile of choice is a domicile voluntarily adopted, the existence of constraints upon the individual's freedom of choice will tend to negate the presumption that a domicile of choice has been acquired. For example, continued political unrest in his home country may compel an individual to reside elsewhere, even for the remainder of his lifetime, but that does not necessarily mean that the country of residence has become the individual's domicile.

3.7 In practice, problems in connection with the acquisition of a domicile of choice most often arise over the requirement as to intention. Clearly, the individual's statements as to his intentions will be relevant, but they are not always conclusive. Although a single factor might in some circumstances be decisive, it is usually necessary to build up an overall picture from a large number of different events and incidents in an individual's life: *Casdagli v Casdagli* [1919] AC 145, 88 LJP 49, HL. Cases coming before the courts have indicated the heavy burden of proof required to show that domicile of origin has been lost and a new domicile of choice has been acquired: *Re Clore (No 2), Official Solicitor v Clore* [1984] STC 609. This observation applies equally to arguments by the Revenue that foreign individuals have acquired a UK domicile of choice: *Buswell v IRC* [1974] 2 All ER 520, [1974] STC 266; *IRC v Bullock* [1976] 3 All ER 353, [1976] STC 409 CA.

Relevant factors

3.8 It is impossible to list all of the factors that could conceivably be relevant in determining domicile. Residence, as well as being a necessary element in acquiring domicile of choice, is also evidence of intention. The manner and extent of residence are important. The more established and extended the residence is, the greater the weight to be attached to it. Nationality, whilst distinct from domicile, is also an important indicator. For example, retention of foreign nationality, despite extended residence in the UK, is consistent with a claim not to have acquired a domicile in the UK. Application for UK citizenship, on the other hand, may indicate an intention to reside indefinitely. Other material factors include the residence in the country concerned of members of the individual's family, cultural connections such as the ability to speak the local language, making a will and appointing locally resident executors, financial or business interests, and involvement in social activities, such as membership of clubs, societies and churches. Even expressing a desire for one's body to be interred in a particular country after death may be relevant, especially if a burial plot is acquired.

3.9 Because an individual may have only one operative domicile at any one time, it follows that the acquisition of a domicile of choice entails relinquishing the immediately preceding domicile, whether it is domicile of origin, of dependency, or of choice. Coupled with the establishment of ties with the new domicile, there must therefore be a breaking of links with the former domicile. The continuance of some existing ties will, in practice, make it more difficult to determine whether the former domicile has been lost. In establishing a particular domicile with a view to obtaining a tax advantage, it is advisable as far as possible to avoid having conflicting connections of this kind.

3.10 In cases where an individual of UK origin takes up residence abroad with a view to acquiring a foreign domicile of choice, practical problems can arise where the country concerned is a federation. If the individual moved from state to state within that country, the UK Revenue might argue that he had not acquired a new domicile of choice. To acquire a domicile of choice, the individual must reside in a particular state and have the intention of residing there permanently. Some of the countries where such problems can arise are the USA, Canada, Australia, South Africa and Switzerland. In any particular case, it is necessary to ascertain whether questions of law, to which – in the UK context – domicile would be relevant, are governed by state or by federal law in the country concerned.

Abandonment of domicile of choice

3.11 Domicile of choice may be lost if the individual ceases to reside in the country concerned either with the intention not to return to reside there indefinitely, or without any definite intention of returning: *Re Flynn, Flynn v Flynn* [1968] 1 All ER 49, [1968] 1 WLR 103. It is not sufficient merely for there to be an intention to reside elsewhere without an actual change of residence: *IRC v Duchess of Portland* [1982] Ch 314, [1982] STC 149. Again, the abandonment of a domicile of choice must be voluntary and not through force of circumstance: *Re Evans, National Provincial Bank v Evans* [1947] Ch 695, [1948] LJR 498.

3.12 If a domicile of choice is abandoned without a acquiring a new domicile of choice, domicile of origin automatically revives as the individual's operative domicile. This is the case regardless of any changes in domicile prior to the individual's attaining full age. Moreover, renewed residence in the domicile of origin is not necessary: *Tee v Tee* [1974] 3 All ER 1105, [1974] 1 WLR 213, CA. Revival of domicile of origin is a particular risk for those of UK origin who have emigrated but return to the UK for an employment assignment or some other reason. It is essential for them to show not only that they have acquired a domicile of choice elsewhere but also that the domicile has not lapsed by virtue of their visits to the UK. Provided that the UK visit is for a temporary reason, and extensive ties are retained with the adopted domicile, the Revenue normally accept that UK domicile has not revived.

Married women

3.13 Since the end of 1973, married women have been able to establish independent domicile, in accordance with the principles already outlined: Domicile and Matrimonial Proceedings Act 1973 s 1(1). Before that, a married woman automatically acquired her husband's domicile (if different from her own) as a domicile of dependence. Women who married before 1974 retain their former domicile of dependence, but as a domicile of choice, capable of being abandoned: DMPA 1973 s 1(2). However, since abandonment of a domicile of choice requires that the individual ceases to reside in the country concerned, reversion to domicile of origin cannot be claimed merely on the grounds of the intention to return there: *IRC v Duchess of Portland* [1982] Ch 314, [1982] STC 149. Similarly, there is no automatic reversion to domicile of origin on the husband's death, or on separation or divorce: *Re Wallach, Weinschenk v Treasury Solicitor* [1950] 1 All ER 199, 66 (pt 1) TLR 132; *Faye v IRC* (1961) 40 TC 103, [1961] TR 297.

3.14 There is an exception to the above rules for US citizens who before 1974 married husbands having UK domicile. Under Article 4(4) of the double taxation convention between the UK and the USA, they are treated as retaining their US domicile of origin provided they can show, on the normal rules, that a domicile of choice has not been acquired elsewhere: Double Taxation Relief (Taxes on Income) (United States of America) Order 1980 SI 1980 No 568.

Deemed domicile: inheritance tax

3.15 For inheritance tax, an individual may be deemed to be domiciled in the UK even though he is not so domiciled in general law. First, an individual is deemed to be UK domiciled if he was actually so domiciled at any time in the period of three calendar years preceding the event giving rise to a potential IHT charge, such as a gift, or death: IHTA 1984 s 267(1)(a). Prior *deemed* domicile (under this rule, or that in **3.16**) does not activate the three year rule. Thus, UK domicile for IHT purposes persists for up to three years after the acquisition of another domicile elsewhere, whether by choice or even, on relinquishing a UK domicile of choice, by reversion to foreign domicile of origin.

3.16 Alternatively, an individual is deemed to be domiciled in the UK for IHT purposes if he has been resident in the UK in at least 17 of the 20 consecutive tax years ending with the tax year in which the gift, or other transfer of value or death occurs: IHTA 1984 s 267(1)(b). Residence has the same meaning as for income tax purposes, except that the existence of available accommodation in the UK is left out of account. In general, therefore, residence will relate to prolonged or repeated visits to the UK (see **2.6**).

3.17 For events occurring before 15 March 1983, additional rules treated certain UK domiciled individuals who had acquired a new domicile in the Channel Islands or the Isle of Man as retaining UK domicile indefinitely. These rules have now been wholly repealed: F(No 2)A 1983 s 12.

3.18 If an individual is deemed to be domiciled in the UK under the foregoing rules, but is not in fact so domiciled, he nevertheless continues to be exempt from IHT on specified UK government stocks (see **1.8**): IHTA 1984 ss 6(2), 267(2).

3.19 The IHT position may be affected by the existence of a double taxation convention on estate and gift taxes between the UK and another country. Even though an individual may be domiciled or deemed to be domiciled in the UK, he may potentially qualify for relief under such a treaty as a national or citizen of the other country. In those circumstances, it will be necessary to resolve his domicile status for the purposes of the treaty, and this is normally done on the basis of 'tie-breaker' rules analogous to those applicable in some income tax treaties. The text of a model domicile article is shown at Appendix 4.

Claims and appeals

3.20 The procedure for claims regarding domicile is identical to that applying in the case of residence and ordinary residence. Claims are made to the Board of Inland Revenue, with right of appeal to the Special Commissioners. As in the case of residence, determination of domicile is largely based upon fact and it is extremely important that all relevant facts are adduced as evidence before the Special Commissioners in the case of any dispute. Moreover, because domicile involves the establishing of an intention, statements made by the individual, whether orally or in writing, regarding his plans as to residence are often crucial. Their importance was illustrated in the *Clore* case, where doubts expressed by Sir Charles Clore to his friends about leaving the UK undermined the contention that he had lost his UK domicile of origin to become domiciled in Monaco, despite his having left the UK to set up a home there and having made a will in Monaco: *Re Clore (No 2), Official Solicitor v Clore* [1984] STC 609.

Proposals for change

3.21 A joint report by the Law Commission and the Scottish Law Commission on the law of domicile was published in April 1985, as a Green Paper, for discussion. The report concluded that, while the concept of domicile should broadly be retained, the rules relating to change of domicile need modification. It was proposed that the doctrine of revival of domicile of origin (see **3.12**) should be abolished and that a person of full age should retain their operative domicile until a new domicile is positively acquired. The report also suggested that a conclusive test for acquisition of a new domicile should be habitual residence in a territory for a period of

7 years or more after reaching full age. Whilst some of the changes proposed would undoubtedly have been of benefit to individuals changing their place of residence on a long term basis, it now seems unlikely that any of the proposals will be proceeded with. It is noteworthy that a Bill to implement similar changes proposed in 1954 by the Private International Law Committee was dropped following pressure from the foreign business community in the UK.

4 Foreign investment by UK residents

4.1 There have been no UK exchange controls since October 1979 and thus there are no official constraints upon investments abroad by UK residents. Individual investors may invest funds where they wish, official consent not being required, and may purchase foreign currency for investment or other purposes at prevailing market rates, without restriction. There is no requirement as to repatriation of either income or capital to the UK. The complete absence of control extends equally to export and import of funds for personal expenditure, and the maintaining of foreign currency bank accounts.

4.2 A major practical consequence of freedom from exchange controls is that foreign investment by UK resident individuals is an everyday event. For example, offshore investment funds of many different kinds have developed and it is commonplace for UK clearing banks to offer their customers a range of foreign currency accounts in addition to the more usual sterling current and deposit facilities. The proliferation of investment media outside the UK has not unnaturally brought with it tax planning opportunities and, inevitably, anti-avoidance legislation.

General tax position

4.3 As already explained (see **1.4**), UK residents are subject to income tax on all their sources of income, wherever arising. Income from investments outside the UK is therefore taxable and is required to be disclosed in an individual's UK tax returns. Similarly, capital gains on the disposal of such investments is subject to CGT. For those not domiciled in the UK, income and capital gains arising outside the UK are taxable only if received in the UK. The definition of what constitutes a remittance is outlined in **1.17**. However, the generality of UK residents who are UK domiciled are taxable on foreign income and gains whether or not they are remitted to the UK. The absence of any requirement to repatriate income and disposal proceeds does not therefore in itself have any effect on the tax liability of UK domiciled residents.

Ordinary residence

4.4 Ordinary residence status has a number of implications for the taxation of foreign investment. Commonwealth and Irish citizens who are not ordinarily resident in the UK are taxable on the remittance basis (see **1.16**): TA 1988 s 65(4). For those who are not UK domiciled, but are ordinarily resident in the UK, the definition of a remittance is extended to include money borrowed abroad and brought to the UK after repaying the debt with the foreign income or gains: TA 1988 s 65(7). As explained in **1.5**, being ordinarily resident in the UK renders an individual liable to CGT, even though for the year in question he is not resident: CGTA 1979 s 2(1).

Basis of assessment

4.5 The tax rules for computing the amount of income assessable for a given tax year differ according to the type of income concerned. The basis of assessment for foreign investment income is, however, uniform. Except where foreign income is received through a UK paying or collecting agent (see **4.23** below), it is chargeable under Schedule D Case IV or V. The differences between Cases IV and V are largely historical, with Case IV covering income from foreign securities, Case V all other foreign source income. The basis of assessment is the same in each case, being the amount of income from the source arising in the preceding tax year: TA 1988 s 65(1). However, investment income arising from sources in the Republic of Ireland is always assessed on the amount arising in the tax year: TA 1988 s 68(1). There are special rules for new and ceasing sources, as explained below. There is an administrative saving in that all income under Case IV and V (as well as UK interest taxable under Case III) may be assessed in one sum: TA 1988 s 73. This does not, however, affect the general principle that each source is distinct and the special rules described below are applied separately to each one.

4.6 For a new source of income, the assessment for the first tax year for which income arises is the amount arising in that year: TA 1988 s 66(1)(*a*). For the following year, the assessment is again on the amount arising in the year: TA 1988 s 66(1)(*b*). In the third year, the preceding year basis applies, unless the taxpayer elects for the current year basis to apply: TA 1988 s 66(1)(*c*). Such an election has to be made within six years of the end of the tax year concerned. If income first arises on 6 April in any year, the following year is assessed on the preceding year basis, with the taxpayer's right to elect for the current year basis (as for year 3 in other cases): TA 1988 s 66(1)(*c*).

EXAMPLE

4.7 PQ acquired shares in SR Inc, a foreign company, in December 1988. Dividends arose as follows:

January 1989	£1,500
February 1990	2,200
February 1991	1,800

	Basis	*Amount*
Year 1: 1988/89	Current year	£1,500
Year 2: 1989/90	Current year	2,200
Year 3: 1990/91	Current year*	1,800
Year 4: 1991/92	Preceding year	1,800

*At taxpayer's option, being lower than preceding year basis.

4.8 Special rules also apply when the source of income ceases. Here, the assessment for the tax year in which the individual ceases to possess the source is on the incoming arising for that year: TA 1988 s 67(1)(c). For the tax year before that in which the source ceases, the assessment is revised from preceding year to current year basis, if higher.

EXAMPLE

4.9 In the preceding example, PQ disposes of the shares in March 1995. Dividends arising are as follows:

March 1993	£4,500
February 1994	£5,200
February 1995	£4,000

Assessments are:

	Basis	*Amount*
Final year: 1994/95	Current year	£4,000
Penultimate year: 1993/1994	Current year*	5,200

*Revised from preceding year basis, which is less.

4.10 Where a source of income does not give rise to income for one or more tax years, it may be possible to elect for the normal rules to modified. First, if no income arises in the last two years of the income source – that is, the year in which it ceases and the immediately preceding year – the taxpayer can elect for the last year in which income arose to be treated at the year in which the source ceased: TA 1988 s 67(1)(c). This will eliminate the assessment on the preceding year basis for the year following that in which income last arose, but may also cause the immediately preceding year's assessment to be increased, as explained in **4.8**. Any elections here have to be made within two years of the end of the tax year in which the source of income ceased.

4.11 The election outlined in **4.10** cannot be made more than eight years after the end of the tax year in which income last arose. However, if an income source does continue for six consecutive tax years or more without any income arising, an alternative election may be made to treat the source as ceasing in the year in which income last arose and as recommencing at the end of the six-year period following that year: TA 1988 s 67(5). The commencement rules will then apply as and when income again arises. The time limit for this election is eight years from the end of the year in which income last arose.

4.12 It may be a matter of some practical importance that income arises at one date rather than another since that will determine the tax year for which the income is assessed. Generally speaking, income arises when it is credited or otherwise made available to the individual entitled to it. Income, such as interest, which accrues over a period does not necessarily arise from day to day but only when credited to the individual's account. There are, however, special rules relating to sales of securities with accrued interest: TA 1988 ss 710–728 (see **4.28**).

4.13 It sometimes happens that income may not freely be dealt with by the UK resident individual; for example, because of foreign exchange controls. In this kind of situation, relief from UK tax may be claimed: TA 1988 s 584. The taxpayer has to show that either the laws of the country where the income arises, or executive action by its government or unavailability of foreign currency there, prevent the transfer of the income to the UK. Delay in the processing of applications to the exchange control authorities concerned is not grounds for a claim. An additional condition is that the income must not have been, despite reasonable endeavours on the part of the taxpayer, converted into sterling outside that country or converted into another currency which is freely remittable to the UK. Relief must be claimed within 6 years of the end of the tax year in which the income arose.

4.14 If a claim is accepted, the income will not be assessed for the year in which it arises until such time as the Revenue judges that it has become freely remittable. The Revenue can then make assessments for the years in which the income arose: TA 1988 s 584(2). This will not necessarily result in the same tax liability that would have arisen had the claim not been made. Translation of foreign currency into sterling is made, not at the rate for the year in which the income arose but at the date when the income is treated by the Revenue as having become remittable. The rate is the market rate or, if there is no quoted rate, the official exchange rate in the foreign country: TA 1988 s 584(8). As an alternative to non-assessment of unremittable income, or where the conditions for relief are not wholly satisfied, there is a facility for suspending collection of tax on such income, with consequent remission of interest on overdue tax: TMA 1970 s 92.

Remittance basis

4.15 Where a UK resident entitled to the remittance basis remits foreign income to the UK, the basis of assessment is analogous to that applying to income taxed on the amount arising: TA 1988 ss 65(5), 66(6), 67(6). In other words, the assessment is normally on the amount remitted in the preceding tax year, with special rules applying to new and ceasing sources. For new sources, the commencement provisions run from the year in which income is first remitted to the UK, which need not be when income first arises. On cessation of a source, the closing rules apply to the last two years of the source, with the possibility of going back to the last year in which remittances were made if no income was remitted in the last two years of the source.

4.16 Translation of income into sterling should be at the rate applicable to the date the remittance is made, although the average rate for the tax year in which it was made seems to be an acceptable alternative in practice. Whichever basis is adopted, it should be applied consistently from year to year. Where the preceding year basis applies, the rate of exchange for the tax year for which the income is assessed will not be relevant. It may happen that the sterling amount of the income arising from the source is less than the sterling amount of remittances, if the foreign currency has appreciated against sterling. It is arguable that the assessable amount should be restricted in these circumstances, since an individual should not be assessed on more income than has actually arisen to him, income for UK tax purposes being always expressed in sterling. However, the conversion of the remitted currency into sterling may give rise to a capital gain, the base cost being the sterling value of the currency at the date the income arose: *Bentley v Pike* [1981] STC 360, 53 TC 590.

4.17 Income for UK tax purposes must have a source within one of the income tax Schedules or Cases, in the tax year concerned: TA 1988 s 1(1). Once the source has ceased, there can be no income from that source. Consequently, if income from a foreign source is remitted after the end of the tax year in which the source ceases, no assessment may be made on that income. Provided that a non-domiciled individual is in a position to delay remittances in this way UK income tax liability can be avoided. Cessation of a source cannot always be easily arranged, but a relatively straightforward case is the closing of a foreign bank deposit account. If the account is closed on 5 April, and the funds are remitted to the UK on 6 April, there will be no UK tax liability on the interest credited to the account.

Sources of income: computation

a Interest

4.18 Interest arising abroad is assessed under Schedule D Case IV if it arises on a secured loan, such as a loan secured on real estate by way of a mortgage: *Singer v Williams* [1921] 1 AC 41, 7 TC 419, HL. Otherwise, assessment is under Case V. Deductions are not in strictness available although the cost of remitting income to the UK is in practice allowed by the Revenue. Income from each source is computed separately, but Case IV and Case V income for the tax year may be aggregated and assessed in one sum: TA 1988 s 73. In principle, each deposit to a bank account is a separate source: *Hart v Sangster* [1957] Ch 329, 37 TC 231, CA. Practically speaking, individual bank accounts are treated as separate sources. A premium on redemption of a foreign loan may be taxable income, depending upon the terms and circumstances of the loan: *Lomax v Peter Dixon & Son Ltd* [1943] KB 671, 25 TC 353, CA. Where securities are sold with accrued interest, there may be an additional tax assessment (see **4.28**).

b Dividends

4.19 Foreign dividends are assessed under Schedule D Case V. A deduction may in practice be given for costs of remitting the dividend to the UK. Whether a dividend constitutes income in the hands of the shareholder may depend upon the provisions of foreign law relating to the payment: *Rae v Lazard Investment Co Ltd* [1963] 1 WLR 555, 41 TC 1, HL. The fact that a dividend may be a distribution of capital profits does not necessarily make it a capital receipt: *IRC v Reid's Trustees* [1949] AC 361, 30 TC 431, HL. The tax treatment of the dividend in the foreign country is not a conclusive factor. It should be borne in mind that receipt of foreign dividends treated as capital for UK tax purposes will constitute a partial disposal of the shares concerned for CGT: CGTA 1979 s 72.

c Rental income

4.20 Income arising from land outside the UK is taxable under Schedule D Case V: *Swedish Central Rly Co v Thompson* [1924] 2 KB 255, 9 TC 342, CA. There are no statutory rules governing the computation of such income but in practice the rules relating to UK rental income are followed. Deductible items therefore include repair and maintenance expenditure, costs of management and rents payable under a head lease. Interest on money borrowed to purchase or improve a property overseas is not deductible against rental income: *Ockenden v Mackley* [1982] 1 WLR 787, [1982] STC 513. Losses arising under Schedule D Case V are strictly speaking not allowable. However losses on foreign property letting may be carried forward against future income from the same property: Extra-statutory concession B25.

d Business investments

4.21 Profits from a business managed and controlled outside the UK are taxable under Schedule D Case V: *Colquhoun v Brooks* (1889) 14 App Cas 493, 2 TC 490, HL. There is no statutory direction on how profits and losses are to be computed, but in practice the rules applicable to Cases I and II are followed. It is unlikely that a UK resident could manage and control a sole proprietorship outside the UK and in practice the profits will often be UK source income: *Spiers v Mackinnon* (1929) 14 TC 386, 8 ATC 197. However, a UK resident's share of profits from a foreign partnership managed outside the UK by non-resident partners will be foreign source income.

e Trust income

4.22 If a UK resident individual has an interest in possession in the income of a foreign trust, the income will be UK or foreign source according to its individual components: *Baker v Archer-Shee* [1927] AC 844, 11 TC 749, HL. Where the beneficiary does not have any interest in possession in income, but receives income paid by virtue of the exercise of the foreign trustee's discretion, the income will be foreign source: *Archer-Shee v Garland* [1923] AC 212, 15 TC 693, HL.

UK paying and collecting agents

4.23 Dividends and interest on foreign shares and securities are often paid to UK residents through an agent. The agent can be a paying agent appointed by the foreign company, or a collecting agent acting on behalf of the recipient. Where the paying agent is in the UK, or there is a UK collecting agent which receives the income, the agent is obliged to withhold income tax from the payment at the basic rate: TA 1988 s 123. An individual's own bank is a collecting agent for this purpose where the foreign dividends etc are credited directly to his account with the bank. However, the Revenue do not regard a UK branch of the overseas company concerned as a UK paying agent. The withholding procedure also applies to income taxable under Schedule C, in respect of securities issued by foreign governments or other public institutions overseas: TA 1988 s 17. Income arising from sources in the Republic of Ireland may be excluded from withholding, provided that the UK paying agent provides the Revenue with full particulars: TA 1988 Sch 3 para 15.

4.24 Although deductions are not in strictness permitted in computing foreign dividend or interest income, the Revenue in practice allow the deduction of

(a) collection charges of an overseas bank;
(b) exchange commissions of up to 0.1%;
(c) collection charges of UK banks of up to 2%;
(d) costs of insurance of coupons.

Foreign dividends etc received through an agent are assessed on a current year basis, with a credit for the tax withheld. No assessment is made unless the individual is taxable at a rate higher than the basic rate. The tax withheld may be partly or fully repaid if the individual is liable to tax on the income at less than the basic rate. As to the treatment of foreign dividends or interest subject to foreign withholding tax, see **4.43**.

Capital gains

4.25 Capital gains on the disposal of foreign investments are calculated according to normal CGT rules. In essence, the gain (or loss) is calculated by reference to the disposal proceeds net of incidental costs of disposal, less the cost of acquiring the asset, including incidental costs of acquisition, less any improvement expenditure of a capital nature: CGTA 1979 s 32. For investments acquired before 1 April 1982, gains or losses are calculated as if their acquisition cost had been their open market value at 31 March 1982: FA 1988 s 96(2). Market value is not substituted if to do so would produce a greater gain or loss: FA 1988 s 96(3) but this restriction can be disapplied by election, which then applies to all assets acquired before 1 April 1982: FA 1988 s 96(5). An indexation allowance is also given for the increase in the UK retail prices index over the period of ownership: FA 1982 s 82. Assets acquired by gift are treated as having a base cost equal to their market value at the date of gift; for inherited assets, probate value is the allowable cost.

4.26 Where disposal proceeds and allowable expenditure are in foreign currency, the amounts are translated into sterling at the exchange rates prevailing on the dates concerned: *Bentley v Pike* [1981] STC 360, 53 TC 590. For an asset owned on 31 March 1982, it would be necessary to use the rate of exchange on that date to translate the foreign currency value into sterling. It is not permissible to calculate the gain or loss in foreign currency and then translate into sterling. A taxable gain may therefore arise even where the investor has broken even or made a loss on disposal.

EXAMPLE

4.26A CD acquired a holiday home in the US when the rate of exchange was $2.20. The property cost $80,000 inclusive. CD sold the property for $75,000 net of expenses, when the exchange rate was $1.72. The indexation factor is assumed to be 0.157.

Disposal proceeds:	$75,000 @$1.72	£43,604
Allowable cost:	$80,000 @$2.20 = £36,363	
Indexation allowance:	0.157 × £36,363 = 5,709	
		42,072
Chargeable gain		£ 1,532

4.27 The tax effects can be particularly harsh where a foreign asset is purchased using borrowed money. If the foreign currency has appreciated against sterling, the sterling equivalent of the loan will have increased. However, no relief is available for the effective exchange loss, because the repayment of a loan is not the disposal of an asset and is thus not within the ambit of CGT.

4.28 The sale of foreign securities with accrued interest may give rise to an income tax liability, instead of or in addition to a liability to capital gains tax. The provisions of the accrued income scheme are complex and a full discussion is outside the scope of present work. Broadly, however, the scheme applies to all securities other than shares, whether the issuer is UK or foreign: TA 1988 s 710(2). Apart from a de minimis exclusion for transferors the nominal value of whose holding does not exceed £5,000 at any time in the tax year: TA 1988 s 715(1)(*b*), the chief exclusion in the present context is for individuals not domiciled in the UK who are taxable on the remittance basis in respect of income from foreign securities: TA 1988 s 715(1)(*j*). Where the accrued income scheme rules do apply, the amount taxable as income is the income accrued from the last interest date up to the date of settlement for the transfer: TA 1988 s 713(2). There is a rebate amount if the securities are sold without accrued income ie ex div: TA 1988 s 713(3), and the rebate amount is deductible from accrued income arising in respect of other securities of the same kind.

4.29 Foreign currency amounts are translated into sterling using the London closing rate for the date of settlement: TA 1988 s 713(9). This may not coincide with the exchange rate used for CGT purposes, which is normally the rate prevailing at the date of the contract to sell. Where a sale or other disposal of foreign securities gives rise to accrued income, the amount of the income is deducted from the chargeable gain arising on the transfer: CGTA 1979 s 33A.

4.30 As already mentioned, foreign currency is itself an asset within the scope of CGT: CGTA 1979 s 19(1)(b). Chargeable gains and allowable losses are computed by reference to the sterling values of the currency at the dates of acquisition and disposal, respectively: *Bentley v Pike* [1981] STC 360, 53 TC 590. Disposal for this purpose generally occurs when the currency is converted into sterling, but can also be the purchase of an asset using the currency or even the deposit of currency in a bank account. Capital gains on foreign currency acquired by an individual for personal expenditure by himself, his family or his dependants outside the UK are, however, exempt from CGT: CGTA 1979 s 133. For this purpose, the cost of providing or maintaining a private residence abroad is treated as personal expenditure.

4.31 Whilst debts are in general exempt from CGT, one exception is a bank account in foreign currency: CGTA 1979 s 135. The account need not be held with a bank outside the UK. Each withdrawal from such an account is a disposal giving rise to chargeable gains or allowable losses. CGT computations drawn up on such a basis could be extremely complex and the Revenue instead accept computations which aggregate all transactions for the year at the appropriate exchange rates: see *'Taxation'* 7 March 1981 p 665. The individual may also opt to aggregate transactions on all foreign bank accounts held by him, ignoring transfers between the accounts: Statement of Practice SP 10/84. An additional practical saving is that foreign currency bank accounts maintained in order to meet personal expenditure outside the UK are exempt and need not be considered: CGTA 1979 s 135(2).

4.32 Non-UK domiciled individuals are taxed only on remittances to the UK of gains on disposals of assets outside the UK, and losses on such assets are not allowable for tax: CGTA 1979, ss 14(1), 29(2). The amount of any remittance is calculated as the sterling equivalent of foreign currency at the date of the remittance, without regard to the exchange rate at the date of the disposal. However, as in the case of income remittances, the amount of the gain actually arising, expressed in sterling, is arguably an upper limit on the sterling amount of remittances that may be taxed. Any foreign currency proceeds remitted and converted into sterling may give rise to a further chargeable gain or allowable loss (see **4.16**).

4.33 The arrangements adopted for income tax, whereby income taxed on the remittance basis is credited to a separate bank account outside the UK, are not fully effective in enabling foreign capital gains to be isolated. Disposal proceeds cannot readily be differentiated between gains and return of original investment, and it is therefore preferable to credit such 'tainted' capital funds to a third bank account. As already noted (see **1.22**), the Revenue take the general approach that remittances out of mixed funds consist first of income, then of capital gains, then of capital. It may be possible to use this argument to 'cleanse' capital gains/capital accounts, by first transferring an amount equal to the net gains to another bank account outside the UK. The balance on the first account can then be regarded as pure capital, and can be remitted to the UK without tax liability. Gains on overseas assets can alternatively be passed through an overseas trust to avoid UK taxation on remittances (see **8.49**). Overseas gains realised when an individual is not domiciled but remitted to the UK after becoming UK domiciled, have been held by the General Commissioners to be taxable.

Foreign taxation

4.34   Although UK tax considerations are important, it should not be forgotten that the country in which income or capital gains arise will often seek to levy tax as well. It is impossible to generalise, since the position will be governed by the tax code of the country concerned. In many cases, non-residents are subject only to a withholding tax at a flat rate, but there will sometimes be a liability to tax at graduated rates. For UK residents, such foreign taxes usually rank for double taxation relief in the UK, provided they are levied on a comparable basis to income tax or CGT. A pure transaction tax calculated on the value of an asset will not be creditable and will usually be allowable only as an expense in calculating UK chargeable gains.

Double taxation relief

4.35   In the absence of a double taxation treaty between the UK and the country where the income or gain arises, double taxation relief is given by crediting the foreign tax against UK income tax on the income or gain concerned: TA 1988 s 790. Relief is not given for tax imposed on UK residents by, say, country A in respect of income arising in country B, (except where country A is the Isle of Man or the Channel Islands). Moreover, the foreign tax must be of the same general character as UK income tax, and not, for example, a capital tax or a registration duty: TA 1988 s 790(12). The Revenue publish a list of creditable taxes, updated from time to time.

4.36   Credit is given only for the foreign tax on the item of income or capital gains tax, and any excess credit cannot be used, either by offset elsewhere or by carry forward. The UK income tax is computed on the gross amount of the foreign income: TA 1988 s 795(1). Credit is given by treating the foreign income as the top slice of the individual's income: TA 1988 s 796(1). For a number of different sources of foreign income which have suffered tax abroad, each time in turn is treated as the top slice, excluding the items already taken into account: TA 1988 s 796(2). In practice, the source having borne the highest rate of foreign tax would be considered first, so as to give overall the most benefit.

EXAMPLE

4.37   For 1991/92, EF has UK investment income of £22,000, and foreign income as follows:

	Gross amount	Foreign tax
Property rental	£ 5,000	£2,500
Interest	£10,000	£1,500

EF is entitled to personal allowances of £5,015.

(a)(i)	Aggregate gross income including foreign sources	£37,000
	Personal allowances	£ 5,015
	Taxable income	£31,985
	Income tax on £31,985	£ 9,239.00
(ii)	Taxable income excluding foreign property rentals	£26,985
(iii)	Income tax on £26,985	£ 7,239.00
	Income tax on foreign rental income	£ 2,000.00
	Credit for foreign tax (maximum)	£ 2,000.00
	Excess credit unutilised	£ 500.00
(b)(i)	Taxable income excluding foreign property rentals	£26,985
	Income tax on £26,985	£ 7,239.00
(ii)	Taxable income excluding all foreign income	£16,985
	Income tax on £16,985	£ 4,246.25
	Income tax on foreign interest	£ 2,992.75
	Credit for foreign (unrestricted)	£ 1,500.00

Total foreign credit: £2,000.00 + £1,500.00 =	£ 3,500.00
Net income tax liability: £9,239.00 − £3,500.00 =	£ 5,739.00

4.38 Income may be taxed in the UK on a basis different from that in the country where it arises, for example, where the UK uses the preceding year basis and the other country assesses on the current year basis. Double taxation relief is then given by crediting foreign tax for the basis year against UK tax for the assessment year: TA 1988 s 790. This rule applies only in the case of unilateral relief; in the case of relief under double taxation agreements, the position depends upon the wording of the relevant article of the agreement: *Duckering v Gollan* [1965] 2 All ER 115, 42 TC 333. In cases where the same income forms the basis for more than one year of assessment, in the opening years of a new source, for example, the foreign tax may be given as a credit more than once: TA 1988 s 804. The total credit cannot exceed the multiple of the foreign tax that is found by dividing the length of the foreign basis period into the total length of the UK periods. If, when the source ceases, the credit given exceeds the actual foreign tax plus any foreign tax not credited because a basis period falls out of account, the excess is clawed back by assessment.

EXAMPLE

4.39 JQ purchased foreign shares in 1988, on which dividends are as follows:

	Gross dividend	Foreign tax
6 June 1988	£ 5,000	£1,000
15 May 1989	£ 6,500	£1,300
2 June 1990	£ 7,400	£1,480
6 July 1991	£ 4,000	£ 800
30 June 1992	£10,000	£2,000
2 July 1993	£11,500	£2,300

The UK tax position is as follows, assuming that unilateral credit applies.

	Case V		UK tax at 40%	Tax credit
1988/89	(CY)	5,000	2,000	1,000
1989/90	(CY)	6,500	2,600	1,300
1990/91	(PY)	6,500	2,600	1,300
1991/92	(PY)	7,400	2,960	1,480
1992/93	(PY)	4,000	1,600	800
1993/94	(PY)	10,000	4,000	2,000
1994/95	(PY)	11,500	4,600	2,300

If JQ sells the shares on 1 February 1994, the assessments are revised as follows:

1992/93	(CY)	10,000	4,000	2,000
1993/94	(CY)	11,500	4,600	2,300

The basis year 1991/92 has now fallen out of account, so that excess credit falls to be clawed back as follows

Credit given for 1989 foreign tax (2 × £1,300)		£2,600
Less: Actual foreign tax	£1,300	
Credit falling out of account	800	2,100
Credit to be clawed back		£ 500

4.40 Where income is taxed on the remittance basis, the amount received in the UK is grossed up at the rate of foreign tax applicable. The gross amount is then subject to UK income tax, with a credit for the foreign tax: TA 1988 s 795(1). Where foreign income is subject to tax at graduated rates, and a partial remittance is made, the grossing-up is in practice calculated at the average rate of foreign tax.

Double taxation agreements

4.41   If there is a double taxation agreement between the UK and the country where income or capital gains arise, the UK resident may be able to claim relief or exemption from foreign tax. The types of relief commonly available are outlined in **1.43**. For the purposes of a tax treaty, it may be necessary to determine residence if the individual is also resident for tax purposes in the other country (see **2.22**). Any foreign tax still remaining payable is available as a credit against UK tax liability in the same way as outlined above for unilateral relief. An important restriction on treaty relief is, commonly, that income taxable on the remittance basis in the UK does not qualify for relief from foreign tax under the treaty except to the extent that it is actually remitted to the UK. This restriction clearly diminishes the UK tax benefits of the remittance basis in many cases, and will influence decisions on whether to set up separate bank accounts as noted in **1.22**.

4.42   In many cases the relief from foreign tax available under a treaty will merely result in a corresponding increase in UK tax liability. However, there is a net benefit where the foreign tax rate would otherwise have exceeded the UK tax rate, as any excess credit could not have been utilised. The reduction or elimination of foreign withholding taxes also constitutes an important cash flow advantage, especially when income is assessed on the UK in the preceding year basis.

4.43   The treatment of foreign tax withheld from overseas dividends or interest received through a UK agent follows the general rules. The gross amount of income is taxable, with a credit for foreign tax. However, the obligation on the UK agent to withhold could impose a cash flow disadvantange on the UK resident recipient, since income tax at the basic rate is deductible from the amount received by the UK agent. In many cases, the withholding requirement is modified so that the UK agent deducts only the difference between the basic rate of income tax and the foreign withholding tax, thus effectively giving a credit for the latter. This procedure applies in the case of dividends or interest arising in one of the territories included in a list held by the Inspector of Foreign Dividends (see Appendix 5). These territories all have a double taxation treaty with the UK. In the case of four countries – Canada, the Netherlands, Sweden and the US – the procedure has statutory authority under regulations. For example, in the case of a US dividend subject to US withholding tax at 15%, the paying agent would deduct a further 10% of the gross amount if the basic rate of income tax is 25%.

Offshore investment funds

4.44   Following the abolition of exchange controls, a number of offshore funds were set up to channel investment by UK residents into UK government stocks, foreign currencies or other media. Such funds accumulated income arising in respect of the underlying assets, with the intention that UK investors could ultimately realise capital gains taxed at a lower rate than income. The funds themselves have generally been organised in a jurisdiction where corporate taxes are minimal. These arrangements were countered by anti-avoidance legislation which taxes as income any capital gains realised on disinvestment: TA 1988 ss 757–764, Schs 27, 28. For this purpose, gains are calculated without the benefit of indexation. Funds may apply for exemption from these rules but they are then required to distribute to investors a substantial part of the income arising. Nevertheless, offshore accumulation funds can still be used to advantage to defer payment of income tax. If realisation of the investment is timed to coincide with a period of non-residence, an absolute tax saving may be achieved. Individuals not domiciled in the UK are taxed only on remittances of gains on disposal of an interest in an offshore fund: TA 1988 s 761(5).

Foreign companies

4.45 It is not an uncommon fallacy that UK income tax and CGT may be avoided by UK residents if they transfer their assets to a company (or trust) located offshore in a tax haven. To the extent that the supposed efficiency of offshore structures lies merely in non-disclosure to the Revenue, that is patently tax evasion and need not be further discussed. However, there are a number of anti-avoidance rules which counter such arrangements in circumstances where the chief, if not the only, motive for the transfer is tax avoidance.

4.46 As regards income tax, a transfer of assets to an offshore company, or indeed to any non-resident or non-domiciled person, is ineffective to the extent that any individual ordinarily resident in the UK retains the power to enjoy income arising to the non-resident, or receives a capital sum derived from that income: TA 1988 s 739. If this provision applies, the whole of the income concerned is assessable on the UK resident. Non-UK domiciled individuals are not taxable if the income would not have been assessed had it arisen to them directly: TA 1988 s 743(3). It is a valid defence to show that the transfer was for bona fide commercial reasons and not for the purpose of tax avoidance: TA 1988 s 741. It should be noted that the Revenue possess extensive powers to require disclosure of information about the setting up of such arrangements, not only from the principals involved, but also from their advisers: TA 1988 s 745.

4.47 These provisions apply only where the UK resident individual who has the enjoyment of the income arising offshore is the original transferor of the assets: *Vestey v IRC* [1980] AC 1148, [1980] STC 10, HL. If this is not the case, then the income is still assessable, but only to the extent that it is actually distributed to UK residents or used to make benefits available to them: TA 1988 s 740. To that extent, the use of an offshore entity may facilitate a useful deferral of income tax. Practically speaking, a foreign trust is a more suitable vehicle for such arrangements than a company.

4.48 As regards capital gains, a foreign company which is closely held does not have any real advantage for UK resident individuals holding its shares. 'Closely held' for this purpose means, inter alia, that control lies in the hands of five or fewer participators, or in the hands of participators all of whom are directors: TA 1988 s 414. Gains realised by the company are apportioned to the shareholders and assessed to CGT in their hands: CGTA 1979 s 15. There is no defence, as in the case of income tax, to the effect that the arrangement does not have tax avoidance as a primary motive, although there is an exclusion for certain transactions by offshore trading companies. Moreover, capital losses are not apportioned, and are not set off against the company's gains before apportionment to the UK shareholders. Non-UK domiciled shareholders are not taxable on apportioned gains.

Foreign trusts

4.49   The transfer of assets to non-resident trustees has the same income tax implications as a transfer to an offshore company (see **4.45**, **4.46** above). Provided that income is not available for the benefit of the transferor, it will be assessed on the beneficiaries only when received in the UK. In a simple case, a UK resident could settle cash on non-resident trustees to invest abroad, with power to accumulate income for the benefit of his infant children. The income would not be subject to income tax during the period of accumulation provided that the settlor reserves to himself no interests in the settled property, and the settlement is irrevocable. The main tax disadvantages of this type of arrangement are that IHT may be payable on the gift in settlement, and also CGT if the gift were to consist of an asset other than cash.

4.50   The CGT treatment of non-resident trusts has in recent years been exploited to achieve significant tax savings through deferral or avoidance of CGT on gains accruing to the trustees. Since 1981, gains accruing to non-resident trustees have been taxable only when capital payments were received by UK resident and domiciled beneficiaries: FA 1981 s 80. Typically, assets of low value but with prospects of growth, eg shares in a private company where there was a possibility of future stock market flotation, were settled, crystallising only a relatively small gain on transfer to the offshore trustees. Gains could be realised later in respect of the assets, but they would not be taxed until payments were made to UK residents. If the beneficiaries had by then shed their UK resident status, CGT could be avoided entirely. Further, existing UK trusts could be made non-resident without any 'exit charge', except for the recapture of gains previously rolled over when assets were transferred to the trustees by the settlor.

4.51   The UK tax benefits likely to flow from the use of an offshore trust are, however, substantially curtailed from 19 March 1991, by comprehensive anti-avoidance legislation: FA 1991 ss 83–92, Schs 16–18. These complex provisions have three main effects:

(a) an exit charge is imposed on a UK resident trust which ceases to be UK resident: FA 1991 s 83. The trustees are deemed to dispose of and immediately reacquire all the assets held subject to the trust, at their then market value. Liability for any CGT falls on the UK trustees, if not paid within 6 months of the due date by the non-resident trustees, but there is an exclusion for former trustees who resigned prior to any proposal to emigrate the trust;

(b) where the settlor, his spouse, any child of either of them, any spouse of a child, or a company controlled by any of them, has an interest in the settlement, capital gains arising to the trustees are treated as arising to the settlor: FA 1991 Sch 16. Trusts set up before 19 March 1991 are not caught unless they are substantially varied, or property is added to them, on or after that date;

(c) the tax charge on capital payments made to UK resident beneficiaries is increased to take account of the period of CGT deferral achieved by the use of the trust: FA 1991 Sch 17. This supplementary charge applies to all offshore trusts, whenever created, but only to capital payments received after 5 April 1992.

4.52 Whilst these fiscal disincentives undoubtedly limit the benefits achievable through the use of a non-resident trust, there may still be individuals whose personal circumstances make the use of such a trust attractive. In the case of assets where the present gain is low, but there are strong prospects for growth, the offshore trust can provide a vehicle for accumulation of capital against the future emigration from the UK of the settlor and/or his family. To that extent, they should be considered in appropriate cases by those who are concerned, for example, about possible future changes in UK taxation, or the reintroduction of exchange controls. Non-resident trusts can also be used by non-UK domiciled individuals to avoid CGT (see **8.49**).

5 The UK resident working abroad

5.1 This chapter considers the position of individuals who, whilst remaining resident in the UK for tax purposes, work abroad during part of the tax year. The tax treatment of self-employed individuals differs from that of employees and is explained separately. The effects of overseas business trips on social security liabilities and pension scheme benefits also require attention, and are analysed below.

Employment income: the foreign element

5.2 Income from employments is taxed under Schedule E, which also covers offices such as directorships. Like Schedule D, Schedule E is divided into Cases, or sub-headings, as follows:

Case I: Employment income for duties performed in or outside of the UK by individuals resident and ordinarily resident in the UK.

Case II: Employment income for duties performed in the UK by individuals who are resident but not ordinarily resident, or who are not resident, in the UK.

Case III: Employment income for duties performed outside the UK and received in the UK by individuals who are resident in the UK (TA 1988 s 19).

Duties performed outside the UK

5.3 It is a question of fact whether an individual's duties are performed in the UK or not. Today, using modern communications techniques, individuals can initiate or carry out transactions in overseas countries without ever leaving the UK. However, this does not seem to affect the basic assumption that the duties are performed where the individual is physically present at the time they are performed. If an office or employment in substance involves the performance of duties outside the UK for a particular tax year, any UK duties which are incidental to the performance of the overseas duties are deemed to be performed abroad: TA 1988 s 132(2). The meaning of 'incidental duties' is explained in **2.10**.

5.4 The duties of seamen and aircrew on a particular voyage may in fact be performed in a number of different countries, or outside the territorial limits altogether. For UK tax purposes, the position is simplified by deeming the duties to have been performed wholly in the UK in certain circumstances, as follows:

(a) on a sea voyage not extending to a port outside the UK (even though partly outside the three mile limit);
(b) (by UK resident crew only) on an air or sea voyage which begins or ends in the UK or, any other voyage touching the UK, on the parts beginning or ending in the UK: TA 1988 s 132(4)(b).

Thus, a UK resident air hostess on a flight from London to New York would be treated as performing her duties for that flight wholly in the UK. On a flight from Zurich to Sao Paulo via London and the Azores, however, only her duties on the Zurich to London and London to the Azores sections would rank as UK duties.

5.5 Individuals holding public office or employment under the Crown are treated as performing all their duties in the UK if their remuneration is payable out of the public revenue of the UK: TA 1988 s 132(4)(a). This includes virtually all civil servants and members of the armed forces who serve abroad: *Graham v White* [1972] 1 All ER 1159, 48 TC 163; *Caldicott v Varty* [1976] 3 All ER 329, [1976] STC 418. However, foreign service allowances paid to Crown employees to compensate for the additional costs of living abroad are tax free: TA 1988 s 319.

5.6 Although the designated areas of the UK continental shelf (the 'UK sector') are not in law part of the UK, certain earnings for duties performed there are treated as earnings in respect of UK duties: TA 1988 s 830(5). Relevant earnings are those for duties in connection with exploration and exploitation of the seabed and subsoil of the UK sector, such as oil and gas exploration and extraction in the North Sea. It is noteworthy that the duties themselves are not deemed to be performed in the UK, so that – for example – performance of such duties has in itself no impact on UK residence status. In strictness, personal allowances are not available to non-residents working in the UK sector, except by claim under TA 1988 s 278 (see **1.24**). However, it is understood that allowances are in practice given where the earnings are submitted to tax withholding under PAYE.

Basis of assessment

5.7 Under Schedule E Case I and II, tax is assessable on the amount of employment income received in the tax year in respect of the employment: TA 1988 s 202A(1)(*a*). For Case III, the basis of assessment is the amount received in the UK in the tax year: TA 1988 s 202A(1)(*b*). Where under Case II it is necessary to determine the amount of remuneration attributable to the UK duties, any apportionment is made in practice by reference to the relevant numbers of days spent performing the duties in the UK and abroad: Statement of Practice SP5/84 para 2. Apportionment is not normally required where the UK and foreign duties are covered by separate contracts.

5.8 For this purpose, it is immaterial that the employment may have ceased (or may not have commenced) at the time the emoluments are received. Emoluments are treated as received when paid or credited to the employee: TA 1988 s 202B(1)(*a*), (*b*). Special additional rules apply to company directors. The time of receipt is the earliest of the date of payment or:

(i) if payment on account is credited in the company's amounts, the date the payment on account is credited;
(ii) if the emoluments for a period (eg the financial year) are determined before the end of the period, the date when the period ends;
(iii) if the emoluments for a period are not determined until after the end of the period, the date they are determined: TA 1988 s 202B(1)(*c*)–(*e*).

5.9 Tax under Case II or Case III of Schedule E is generally of relevance to individuals coming from abroad to work in the UK, as discussed in detail in chapter 8. Liability under Case II also extends to individuals who cease to be UK resident but continue to work in the UK (see **7.5**). The remittance basis under Case III is available to non-UK domiciled individuals resident and ordinarily resident in the UK under a separate contract with a non-UK resident employer for duties outside the UK: TA 1988 s 192(1). Subject to those qualifications, the generality of UK resident employees and directors are within Schedule E Case I, and are hence subject to income tax on the whole of their remuneration, wherever their duties are performed. However, a special deduction may apply in relation to absences abroad on business (see **5.28**), and there is tax relief for certain expenses connected with overseas assignments.

Expenses and benefits

5.10 For shorter or intermittent absences from the UK, one of the main tax concerns is to ensure that expenses connected with the overseas trips are tax deductible. However, avoidance of income tax on such expenses should not be seen as a tax incentive for individuals working abroad but as the elimination of tax disincentives as compared with working in the UK. The following paragraphs give a brief outline of the basic rules, by way of general background.

5.11 The fact that an individual may perform part of the duties of his employment outside the UK does not in itself affect the principles governing the taxation of benefits and expense reimbursement. In addition to cash remuneration – whether described as salary, bonus, fees or otherwise – employees and directors are also taxed on 'money's worth'. Money's worth includes the monetary value of benefits in kind that can be converted into money (such as property transferred to the employee) or used as money (such as cash vouchers). Personal liabilities of the employee met by the employer also count as money's worth, such as personal community charge for a property occupied by the employee: *Nicoll v Austin* (1935) 19 TC 531, 14 ATC 172 and income tax on his earnings: *Hartland v Diggines* [1926] AC 289, 10 TC 247, HL. If, for example, an employer agreed to compensate an employee for foreign taxes imposed on his earnings, the amount paid would be additional remuneration subject to UK income tax.

5.12 In addition, employees earning £8,500 a year or more, and all directors (with a few minor exceptions) are subject to tax on:

(a) reimbursement of expenses by the employer; and
(b) benefits in kind made available to the employer, in addition to those that would in any case be taxable as money's worth. Such benefits include property which continues to be owned by the employer but which is placed at the disposal of the employee. Common examples are company cars and company housing. Services provided, such as free medical insurance, are also taxable benefits.

Amounts under (a) and (b) are included for the purposes of the £8,500 limit: TA 1988 s 167(2).

5.13 Generally speaking, the amount of a taxable benefit under (b) is the cost to the employer of providing it, except where the benefit consists of the use of property owned by the employer. Here, the benefit is equal to the annual value of the property. For company cars, car fuel, and mobile telephones, a set scale applies. The annual value of living accommodation is the rent that would be obtainable on a letting where the tenant bore the rates and other occupier's taxes, and the landlord met all the costs of insurance, repairs and maintenance: TA 1988 s 837. For properties in the UK, the annual value is the net annual value formerly adopted for rating purposes. The 1984/85 rating revaluation in Scotland is ignored for this purpose: IR Press Release 23 July 1985. Following the abolition of domestic rates and their replacement by the community charge (in 1989 in Scotland and in 1990 in England and Wales), the rating lists are no longer maintained. The Revenue have said that, until an alternative basis is introduced, estimated 'rateable' values will be used, subject to agreement with the District Valuer. If the accommodation is rented by the employer, the lease rental is substituted for the annual value, where – as is usual – it is greater. The additional benefit arising in respect of properties costing more than £75,000 is explained in **9.14**. Any amounts paid by the employee for provision of a benefit are deducted from the taxable amount.

5.14 The deduction of expenses from employment income is extremely restricted. Only the following are deductible:

(a) necessarily incurred costs of travelling in the performance of the duties of the employment; and
(b) the cost of keeping and maintaining a horse to enable the employee to perform the duties of the the employment; and
(c) other amounts expended wholly, exclusively and necessarily in the performance of the duties of the employment: TA 1988 s 198(1).

Thus, with the archaic exception of horse expenses, expenses must be incurred *in the performance of* the employment duties if they are to be deductible. It is not sufficient to show that incurring the expense enabled the employee to perform those duties. For this reason, any costs of a personal nature, such as housing expenses or home to work travel expenses, are not deductible. Subsistence expenses in respect of business trips away from home are normally allowable even though there is an element of personal benefit involved.

Overseas assignments

5.15 For an employee who is both resident and ordinarily resident in the UK, the mere fact of going abroad on a business trip does not affect the UK tax treatment of his remuneration package. Salary and benefits in kind continue to be taxable. Even on an extended absence from the UK, there is normally no reduction in the taxable amount of benefits made available in the UK. For example, living accommodation provided in the UK would be taxable on the full annual benefit (see **5.13** and **9.14**) plus other expenses paid, even though unoccupied for part of the year. It might be possible to reduce the tax charge by limiting availability of the accommodation but practically speaking this would be inconvenient for employees, who would have to remove their personal effects from the property every time they were sent overseas. If an employee or director is provided with a company car which he does not take abroad with him, a tax saving can be achieved for longer absences but only if the car is withdrawn for those periods: TA 1988 Sch 6 para 2.

5.16 Expenses paid and benefits made available outside the UK will also be included in the taxable remuneration of the employee, assuming that he earns £8,500 a year or more or is a director. There is a specific exemption for the cost of medical treatment abroad whilst the employee is on an overseas assignment, and the cost of medical insurance for overseas trips: TA 1988 s 155(6). It may be possible to deduct the amount of benefit or expense but the position depends upon the contractual arrangements and the duration of the overseas trips. A car provided to the employee for use while abroad would be a taxable benefit if it were available for private use. It also appears that, if the individual also has a company car in the UK, the UK car will be treated as a second car for the period abroad and the taxable value will be increased by 50% for that period: TA 1988 Sch 6 para 5(3). This makes it even more advantageous for the UK car to be withdrawn whilst the employee is abroad.

5.17 Under the general rule for deduction of expenses, the costs of travel from the UK to an overseas work location should be deductible where both the UK and the overseas duties are performed as part of a single contract of service. In this circumstance, the costs are incurred in the performance of the employer's duties. Where the employee starts his journey from home it is debatable whether the costs of travel to the UK point of departure – the airport or seaport – are deductible, although the specific rules for overseas travel costs (see **5.18**) should usually obviate any difficulties. Expenses in connection with overseas travel to attend conferences abroad may be disallowed, and hence taxed on the employee, unless it can be shown that attending is part of the employee's duties: *Owen v Burden* [1972] 1 All ER

356, 47 TC 476, CA. It may be difficult to do so where the conference is purely of an instructional nature and similar facilities are available in the UK. However, this is a grey area, and it is often the case that attendance at an overseas conference does form part of the employee's duties – for example, where the employer's business can be promoted, or there is contact with overseas technical specialists working in the same area.

5.18 There are also specific statutory provisions which extend the relief for overseas travel expenses in connection with duties performed partly in the UK and partly abroad. Such expenses are deductible if the travel facilities are provided at the employer's cost or are paid for by the employee and specifically reimbursed: TA 1988 s 194(1), (3). The relief does not apply to travel expenses paid out of inclusive salary, or out of a round sum travel allowance. These rules remove any doubt about 'home to airport' costs, because they relate to the costs of travel from any place in the UK to the overseas station, and similarly to any place in the UK on the return. A limitation is placed on relief under s 194(1), by reference to the actual duties performed abroad:

(a) the duties concerned must be able to be performed *only* outside the UK;
(b) the outward journey must be wholly and exclusively for the purpose of performing the overseas duties, and the return journey wholly and exclusively for the purpose of returning after performing them: TA 1988 s 194(4).

5.19 The main practical effect of this limitation is in relation to overseas conferences where the subject matter could equally well have been presented in the UK, or overseas trips for business which are partly for non-business purpose eg a holiday provided by the employer in conjunction with an overseas business visit. If such travel costs are thereby excluded from s 194(1), they are not necessarily wholly disallowable but a deduction could still be sought under the more stringent general rule of s 198. This would, at best, be likely to result in a disallowance of 'home to airport' costs and an apportionment of the remaining costs if the travel had a dual purpose.

5.20 It is debatable whether the limitation applies also to visits to the employee's home in the UK during an extended overseas trip. There is an implication that the performance of the overseas duties must be complete when the return journey is made, and arguably this is not the case if the employee is merely returning home for a few days eg at the weekend. Any potential difficulty is, however, academic since there is a further specific relief which covers such journeys. To qualify, the employee must be absent from the UK for the purpose of performing the duties of one or more employments: TA 1988 s 194(5). There is a limitation on relief in that:

(a) the duties concerned must be such that they can be performed only outside the UK;
(b) the employee's absence from the UK must be wholly and exclusively for the purpose of performing the overseas duties: TA 1988 s 194(6).

Otherwise, there is no restriction on the number of return visits to the UK, so that relief would extend, for example, to regular weekend visits by an employee stationed abroad temporarily. This relief also applies to absence abroad for the purpose of overseas duties performed under a separate contract (see **5.24**).

5.21 The travel costs of an accompanying spouse will not normally be allowable: *Maclean v Trembath* [1956] 2 All ER 113, 36 TC 653. It might be possible to obtain a tax deduction if the spouse played an essential part in the business trip, such as entertaining potential customers, but the Revenue take a generally tough line on this issue. If the spouse accompanies the employee for health reasons, a deduction may be given: Extra-statutory Concession A5(c).

5.22 The cost of certain family visits to employees stationed abroad is not taxable where the foreign assignment is for a continuous period of 60 days or more (not necessarily under a separate contract): TA 1988 s 194(2). The expenses must be paid directly by the employer or reimbursed to the employee. The return journeys which qualify are those by a spouse and children aged under 18, either accompanying the individual at the beginning of the assignment or for a visit during the course of the overseas tour. The cost of return journeys home by the employee at the end of a 60 day tour of duty abroad are tax-deductible if they are made to visit his family. The maximum allowable number of qualifying return journeys is 2 per person per tax year, although there is no maximum per overseas assignment. No deduction is given for subsistence costs of the family while at the foreign station.

5.23 Subsistence expenses incurred on overseas trips should also be tax deductible where there is a single contract, because they are incurred in the performance of the employee's duties. In practice, difficulties tend to arise where an overseas assignment involves a prolonged stay in the same location. In these circumstances, the Revenue often seek to disallow such expenses on the grounds that they are merely normal living expenses which the employee would otherwise have incurred had he remained in the UK. The rule of thumb appears to be that living expenses are tax deductible only where the assignment is for six months or less, but not for any subsequent periods.

5.24 Where an employee works abroad under a separate contract, the general rules regarding expenses would normally preclude deduction of travelling and overseas subsistence costs because the travelling is not in the performance of the duties of either employment. In these circumstances, the cost of the journey from the UK to the foreign station on commencement of the assignment, and back to the UK on its completion, is specifically allowable: TA 1988 s 193(3). Partial disallowance applies if the journeys were partly for other purposes, such as a vacation. The cost allowable includes travel from the employee's home (if this is the starting point in the UK) to the point of departure, and similarly on the return journey. Relief also applies to the costs of travelling to the UK and back to the overseas station during a period of absence from the UK for the purpose of performing employment duties abroad: TA 1988 s 194(5) (see **5.20**).

5.25 Subsistence expenses of an overseas employment may also be deductible:TA 1988 s 193(4). In this case, the costs have either to be met directly by the employer or met by the employee and reimbursed to him. No deduction is available if the employee is given a round sum allowance or cost of living allowance to meet such expenses or if he meets the expenses out of an inclusive salary. If the employee is accompanied by members of his family, no deduction is available for the cost of their board and lodging, which is a taxable benefit where paid for or reimbursed by the employer. The Revenue have been known to take a strict line on such expenses, arguing that the allowable costs of accommodation should be restricted to the costs that would have been incurred had the employee not been accompanied by his family.

5.26 Additional tax relief is given for travel costs relating to journeys between different work stations abroad where each is governed by a separate service contract: TA 1988 s 193(5). The deduction is given against remuneration from the destination assignment. This may be of benefit, for example, where an individual is a director of a number of different foreign companies, visiting each business location in turn on an extended overseas trip.

Longer absences

5.27 As explained in **2.16**, an overseas assignment involving absence from the UK for a period including a complete tax year will normally result in the individual's becoming non-resident for the whole period. However, if the period of absence does not span a whole tax year, the employee remains UK resident, even where the period exceeds twelve months. Alternatively, the employee's continuing duties in the UK, coupled with retention of a private residence, may mean that he remains UK resident (see **2.7–2.10**). In such circumstances, it may still be possible for the employment earnings to be free of UK tax, provided certain conditions are satisfied.

5.28 Individuals who are resident and ordinarily in the UK, so that their employment earnings are taxable under Schedule E Case I, may claim a deduction equal to 100% of the earnings attributable to a period of absence from the UK of at least 365 days: TA 1988 s 193(1). It is not necessary for there to be a separate contract for duties performed overseas, and the performance of UK duties during the period does not in itself preclude such a claim. A qualifying period may consist wholly of days of absence from the UK, or days of absence plus days spent in the UK, subject to specified limits, as follows:

(a) no single period in the UK may exceed 62 days continuously;
(b) at the date of any arrival in the UK during the qualifying period, the total number of days spent in the UK since the period began must not exceed one sixth of the total period: TA 1988 Sch 12 para 3(2).

5.29 The second of these two requirements is more restrictive than the corresponding limit of 183 days (or 90 days a year on average) for the purposes of determining residence status. In practical terms, an unplanned or unexpected visit to the UK – for whatever reason – can break the qualifying period, so that counting towards the 365 day minimum has to begin again. Clearly, it is not always possible to avoid such visits but where timing is flexible, careful planning can yield substantial benefits.

EXAMPLE

5.30 HC is an engineer working for an oil company. He is posted to Indonesia for a 16-month tour of duty and his home visits are as follows:

		Number of days
Leaves UK for Indonesia	19 8 90	118
Returns to UK on vacation	15 12 90	31
Leaves UK for Indonesia	15 1 91	16
Returns to UK for grandfather's funeral	31 1 91	7
Leaves UK for Indonesia	7 2 91	315
Returns to UK	19 12 91	

At 31 January 1991:

Number of days spent in UK since 19 August 1990:	31
Total number of days since 19 August 1990:	165

Since 31 exceeds one sixth of 165, the period is broken at 15 December 1990 and counting begins again on 15 January 1991. As a result, the qualifying period is only 338 days and no deduction is due.

5.31 There is in general no relief if the 100% deduction is lost as a result of an unforeseen return to the UK, even if it is occasioned by civil unrest or military action in the country where the employee is working. However, an exception is made for any employee who was present in Kuwait or Iraq at any time during the inclusive period 2 June 1990 to 2 August 1990, and whose duties were to be performed to a substantial extent in those countries: FA 1991 s 46. A special relief is available where such an employee returned to the UK after being in Kuwait or Iraq during the period without having completed a qualifying period abroad of at least 365 days. If the 365 day qualifying period would in all probability have been concluded but for the events leading up to and resulting from the invasion of Kuwait on 2 August 1990, all or part of the period of absence may be treated as a qualifying period of at least 365 days. This relief covers the cases where the employee returns less than 365 days after his departure from the UK as well as cases where the unforeseen return causes the 1/6th limit to be exceeded. Special relief would not need to be claimed if, for example, the employee were posted elsewhere abroad after returning to the UK and thereby succeeded in completing the 365 day qualifying period by a further absence abroad.

EXAMPLE

5.32 ZZ left the UK on 1 November 1989 to work for his UK employer on an 18 month contract in Kuwait. He returned to the UK on leave on 13 April

1990 and went back to Kuwait on 30 April 1990. Following the invasion of Kuwait, ZZ crossed the border into Saudi Arabia and arrived back in the UK on 24 August 1990. On September 1990, ZZ was sent by his employer to Nigeria for 6 months. He returned to the UK on 23 December 1990, left for Nigeria on 4 January 1991 and returned home at the end of the contract on 1 May 1991.

		Number of days
Left UK	1.11.89	163
Returned to UK	13. 4.90	
Left UK	30. 4.90	17
Returned to UK	24. 8.90	116
Left UK	30. 9.90	37
Returned to UK	23.12.90	84
Left UK	4. 1.91	12
Returned to UK	1. 5.91	117

On ZZ's return to the UK on 24 August 1990, his period of absence from the UK (including the return visit in April 1990) was 296 days. The number of days spent in the UK during that period was less than 62 days and less than 1/6th of the total. However, if ZZ had not left the UK again, he would not have completed a 365 day qualifying period and so the special relief could have been claimed on the grounds that the contract was for 18 months.

Because of his re-posting abroad, ZZ completed a total period of absence of 547 days, and the 1/6th rule is not breached at any time, so that all his earnings for the period qualify for the 100% deduction.

5.33   For the purpose of the 100% deduction a day of absence from the UK must involve absence at midnight on that day: TA 1988 Sch 12 para 4. It is normally assumed that absence at midnight is sufficient to make the day a day of absence but this is doubtful. In practice, the Revenue do not seem to take the point and regard a transit through the UK as a day of absence where the inbound and outbound journeys are in the same day. However, a day trip from the UK is definitely not a day of absence: *Hoye v Forsdyke* [1981] 1 WLR 1442, [1981] STC 711. A day trip to the UK from abroad may be a day of absence, provided the individual departs before midnight.

5.34   As already noted, the whole of the earnings for a qualifying period attracts the 100% deduction, even though part of them relates to UK duties. In addition, earnings for a period of terminal leave will qualify for the deduction if the leave relates to a qualifying period of 365 days or more : TA 1988 Sch 12 para 3(3). A period of terminal leave taken abroad may in practice be counted towards the 365 day minimum, although strictly the position is doubtful. It may sometimes happen that a UK resident will become non-resident during a qualifying period. This does not automatically terminate the period, and days of absence from the UK after becoming non-resident still count towards the 365 day requirement even though the earnings arising after ceasing to be resident do not qualify for the deduction. The converse applies where a non-resident becomes UK resident but continues to spend time abroad.

5.35 The rules which determine whether the duties of seamen and aircrew are performed in the UK (see **5.4**) are modified for the purposes of the 100% deduction. Duties are treated as performed outside the UK on

(a) any voyage beginning or ending outside the UK, except for any part of the voyage beginning and ending in the UK;
(b) any part of a voyage which begins or ends outside the UK, notwithstanding that the voyage as a whole begins and ends in the UK: TA 1988 Sch 12 para 5.

The purpose of these rules is to enable such duties to count as overseas duties so that the employment is eligible for the 100% deduction. The restrictions on visits back to the UK are modified, in that seafarers (but not aircrew) may spend up to 183 days continuously in the UK without terminating the qualifying period. The one-sixth limit is increased to one-half in the case of seafarers: TA 1988 Sch 12 para 3(2A). (From 1988/89 to 1990/91, the limits were 90 days and one-quarter, respectively). For seafarers, the special relief for workers in Kuwait or Iraq (see **5.31**) is modified to apply to any seafarers in those countries in the inclusive period 5 May 1990 to 2 August 1990: FA 1991 s 46(4).

5.36 Those working in the UK sector (see **1.9**) are deemed to receive emoluments for duties performed in the UK: TA 1988 s 830(5). Although this does not amount to the same thing as saying that the duties are performed in the UK, the Revenue in practice take the view that the 100% deduction cannot be claimed for UK sector duties. However, it would appear that if the employee also works outside the UK sector, the existence of overseas duties cannot be disputed and the employment could therefore qualify for the deduction. Because the UK sector is not part of the UK, days spent in the UK sector still count as days of absence from the UK. For seamen and aircrew, the UK sector is treated as part of the UK, so that duties on voyages from the mainland to UK sector installations are UK duties: TA 1988 Sch 12 para 5.

5.37 Provided that the 100% deduction is available, there are advantages in remaining UK resident rather than becoming non-resident, as follows:

(a) personal allowances may be claimed;
(b) relief or exemption from foreign tax may be claimed under UK tax treaties;
(c) qualifying life assurance premiums (on pre-14 March 1984 policies) may continue to be paid net of tax relief at 12.5%;
(d) withholding tax is not applied to UK rental income.

The main disadvantages of remaining resident are that foreign investment income remains subject to UK income tax and the individual continues to be subject to CGT. There is no facility for tax-free investment in UK gilt-edged stock, assuming that the individual continues to be UK ordinarily resident as well.

Self-employed individuals

5.38 Individuals who are self-employed are not entitled to any special reliefs or deductions in respect of periods spent outside the UK. The general rule is that any expenses incurred wholly and exclusively for the purposes of the business are allowable, so that travel and associated subsistence expenses will normally be tax deductible. Subsistence costs for an extended stay in a single location may however be disallowed on the grounds that they are primarily for the personal benefit of the individual. A UK resident who is a partner in an overseas firm should be able to deduct costs of travel to the overseas location provided that the business is also carried on in the UK. If the business is carried out solely abroad, a UK resident partner is unlikely to be able to deduct the costs of travel to the place of business since these will effectively be 'home to work' travel costs. Unlike employees, the self-employed cannot claim a 100% deduction for lengthy periods of absence from the UK.

Foreign tax

5.39 UK residents working abroad often come within the jurisdiction of foreign taxing authorities. Whether tax is in fact imposed on their earnings or other income depends in large part upon the detailed tax rules of the country concerned, as they apply to the individual's particular circumstances. As a practical matter, it would be impossible within the context of the present work to attempt any meaningful survey of foreign tax systems, and the intention here is to outline the general considerations.

5.40 The first question to be addressed is whether the individual has become a resident of the foreign country. Retention of UK resident status is no bar to being a foreign resident. The criteria of tax residence in the other country may well be different from those in the UK, and the tax year is unlikely to coincide with the UK tax year. Becoming resident will normally make a difference to the basis of taxation and the ability to claim personal allowances and other deductions.

5.41 Any foreign tax charged will, on the assumption that the employee remains UK resident, be credited against his UK income tax liability on that source of income, as described in **4.35**. If the effective rate of foreign tax is higher than the corresponding UK rate, the excess foreign tax will not be creditable and will be a net additional cost to the employee. Even where the nominal foreign tax rate does not differ markedly from the UK rate, the actual tax suffered may still be greater, because of differences in the basis of assessment or method of computing income. Certain expenses, for example, may not be deductible under the foreign tax law. Clearly, where the UK employee is entitled to the 100% deduction in the UK, any foreign tax charged on the earnings will not be creditable in the UK.

5.42 Relief from foreign tax may be available where the UK has negotiated a comprehensive double taxation agreement with the country concerned.

Tax treaties vary in detail, but most now follow a standard format. UK treaties with developed countries tend to follow the OECD model, whilst those between the UK and less developed countries follow the UN model treaty. For employment income, the country of residence has sole taxing rights, unless duties of the employment are performed in the other country, which may then tax the earnings attributable to those duties. However, the earnings are not taxable in the country where duties are performed if:

(a) the employee is present in that country for less than 183 days;
(b) the employment is with a person resident outside that country (but not necessarily resident in the country where the employee is resident);
(c) the earnings are not charged to and claimed as a tax deduction by a permanent establishment of the employer in that country.

All three conditions must be satisfied for exemption to apply. Under (c), a recharge of earnings to an affiliated company in the country concerned does not necessarily negate the exemption.

5.43 If the employee becomes a resident of the other country, whilst remaining UK resident, residence status for the purposes of the treaty must be resolved, and this is normally done as explained in **2.23**.

Tax protection

5.44 If a UK employer sending employees abroad undertakes to compensate them for foreign tax, any additional payments made to achieve that object are subject to UK income tax as already indicated (see **5.11**). There are in practice two main methods of compensating employees for foreign tax. The first, normally referred to as tax protection, is simply to meet any foreign tax liability to the employee, regardless of his UK tax position. An alternative method is to maintain the employee's net after tax income, leaving aside any foreign cost of living allowances, at the same level as it would have been had he remained in the UK. This method is called tax equalisation. In practice, the position will depend upon the exchange rate used, cost of living differentials and allowances made for additional costs such as housing, expatriate schools and so on. In principle, the employee's gross earnings could even diminish if foreign tax is less than the UK 'stay-at-home' tax. The foreign tax effect of tax protection or equalisation also needs to be considered as this may itself increase the foreign tax liability.

EXAMPLE

5.45 AB is a project manager for a UK construction company. He is relocated to South America for a 2 year period. AB's UK salary and benefits package for 1991/92 totals £56,000.

5.45 *The UK resident working abroad*

UK: Remuneration		£56,000	£56,000
Allowances (say)			5,000
Taxable salary			£51,000
Tax thereon	£16,845		
National Insurance	1,635	18,480	
Net after tax		£37,520	

Tax is charged in the country where AB works at a flat rate of 30% on earnings.

If AB's contract with his employer provides that AB will receive £56,000 net, the employer will therefore have to pay him £80,000, on which tax is £24,000. He will effectively be tax protected. (If AB remains UK resident, UK tax might need to be taken into account.)

If there is tax equalisation, AB will receive £37,520 (ignoring any cost of living adjustment or special allowances) and the employer will therefore pay him £53,600 gross.

Social security and benefits

5.46 The national insurance contribution (NIC) liability of an employee is not normally affected by visits abroad, except where such visits are extended, involving loss of UK resident status. Even where the 100% deduction applies for income tax, NICs are still payable. Nevertheless, there may also be a liability to pay foreign social security contributions, regardless of continuing NIC liabilities. Unless there is a bilateral social security arrangement, usually referred to as a totalisation agreement, there is no relief from foreign contributions and they cannot be credited against NIC liability or count towards UK benefits. Under a totalisation agreement, the UK employee would remain liable only to NICs although only where he remained in the employment of a UK resident employer. The most comprehensive agreement is between the UK and the US: The Social Security (United States of America) Order 1984 SI 1984 No 1817, which provides for continuing liability for UK contributions, and exemption from US contributions, for up to five years. The five year period may be extended by up to a further year by agreement. Other reciprocal agreements exist, but provide relief only for relatively short periods in the other country, liability normally arising under the laws of the territory where the employee to working. Different arrangements apply within EC member states, as explained in **7.57**.

Pension arrangements

5.47 An individual who is a member of a UK occupational pension scheme is entitled to continue within the scheme notwithstanding any absences from the UK. Provided that he continues to be employed by a UK employer (or an affiliated UK company in the case of a group scheme) it is immaterial whether he remains UK resident. Scheme membership is unaffected by entitlement to the 100% deduction, although no tax relief will then be available for his contributions. However, UK pension scheme contributions may well not be deductible for foreign tax purposes.

5.48 If the employee's foreign service involves employment by a non-UK resident person, membership of the UK pension scheme may continue only if:

(a) the UK employer and the foreign employer are sufficiently closely associated. For companies, a 51% subsidiary relationship would satisfy this condition; and
(b) the employee remains UK resident and his earnings do not attract the 100% deduction (IR12 para 17.8).

Where these conditions are not satisfied, the part of the scheme relating to the excluded employees is deemed to be a separate unapproved scheme, and an actuarial valuation of the corresponding fund is required: IR12 para 17.2.

5.49 In practice, partial exemption of the pension fund is avoidable, by seconding the employee to the non-UK resident employer. If the period of secondment is to exceed three years, the approval of the Inland Revenue Superannuation Funds Office is required. It will be necessary to show that the UK employer retains control over the employee's movements. Where there is a secondment, the foreign employer is required to reimburse the UK employer for contributions paid into the pension fund for the employee concerned. This may create problems at corporate level for the foreign employer in obtaining a tax deduction for the amounts reimbursed.

5.50 If an employee is not in pensionable employment, he is entitled to make superannuation arrangements through a personal pension scheme. Such schemes require Inland Revenue approval and it is necessary that the employee has relevant earnings within Schedule E for any tax year in which a contribution is made: TA 1988 ss 640, 644. If the employee is not chargeable to tax on his earnings, whether as a result of the 100% deduction or otherwise, the effect of the contribution limit is that no contribution may be made to an approved personal pension scheme, and any contribution made has to be returned by the pension fund: TA 1988 s 638(3). To that extent, a personal pension scheme may in some cases be less flexible for the expatriate than an occupational pension scheme.

Visas and work permits

5.51 Employees working outside the UK will often require a visa in order to enter a particular country and a work permit in order to take up paid work there. For short overseas visits remaining in the employment of a UK employer, work permits will not normally be required, although visa restrictions will often be imposed on the employee's activities. Details of visa and work permit requirements are obtainable from the embassy or consular office of the country concerned. Although in many cases travel agents will handle visa applications, personal attendance at the embassy may be required. UK nationals do not require visas or work permits for visits to other EC member states but a residence permit must normally be obtained for an extended stay.

6 Longer term expatriates

6.1 This chapter explains the tax implications for individuals who cease to be UK resident, either as a result of employment outside the UK or for other reasons. The tax issues specific to overseas employees are considered in detail in chapter 7. The immediate consequence of shedding UK residence is freedom from UK income tax on income arising abroad, and possibly also from CGT, with evident advantages to the individual concerned. Nevertheless, not all the tax consequences of becoming non-UK resident are uniformly beneficial, especially where there are continuing interests in the UK. A detailed review of the departing individual's financial position is essential if the potential benefits are to be maximised and the pitfalls avoided.

Departure from the UK

6.2 The principles and practice that govern changes of residence are set out in chapter 2. Employees working outside the UK cease to be resident and ordinarily resident on the day following departure provided the absence encompasses at least one complete tax year (see **2.16**). Other emigrants cease to be resident on leaving the UK only if there is evidence of a permanent change of residence or, in hindsight, they were absent from the UK for at least 36 months after they departed (see **2.15**).

6.3 Where the conditions necessary for the Revenue practice to be applied are not satisfied, residence status will be decided on a year-by-year basis, on the criteria explained in **2.14** to **2.16**. In the latter circumstances, it is important to note that, although the individual may cease to be UK resident for a year or more, he will not necessarily cease to be ordinarily resident for those years. A potential liability to CGT on asset transfers may therefore persist, despite the evident practical difficulties the Revenue might experience in monitoring transfers made outside the UK.

Personal allowances

6.4 Non-residents are not entitled to claim personal allowances, except on the basis as described in **1.24**: TA 1988 s 278. However, for the year of departure, the full amount of allowances may be claimed, without any abatement for the fact that the individual has not been UK resident for the whole tax year: IR20 para 78. The date of departure, where capable of being planned, can therefore be timed to give a modest but useful UK tax benefit. If departure is early in the tax year, the full year's allowance may be capable of offset against only a fraction of the year's taxable income.

Husband and wife

6.5 As mentioned in **1.33**, married couples are treated in the same way as single persons and the wife's income is not aggregated with that of her husband. Their residence status need not be the same, for example, where one of them remains in the UK whilst the other is abroad for an extended period of employment. However, it can happen that one will remain resident even where both are abroad. For example, a wife might accompany her husband on an overseas assignment, although she retained living accommodation in the UK and visited the UK during the year. Although the husband might be non-resident, because of the statutory disregard of available accommodation held by employees working wholly overseas, the wife would be resident under the normal rules (see **2.7**). Indeed, it might be of benefit for her to remain resident if she had UK source investment income, since she might otherwise not be entitled to claim personal allowances against the income.

6.6 There is scope for tax planning where a husband and wife living together do not have the same residence status. In relation to income tax, transfers of cash or other investments can be made to the non-resident spouse, for reinvestment outside the UK. Income arising to the non-resident would not then be subject to UK income tax. The benefits obtainable in practice depend in addition on the tax regime (if any) overseas to which the non-resident spouse is subject.

6.7 The other main opportunity for UK tax planning relates to CGT. Investments showing a significant accrued gain may be transferred to the non-resident spouse, without tax charge, and sold free of CGT. Care is required to ensure that the transferee's non-resident status is unassailable. In particular, it is inadvisable to rely on the Inland Revenue practice on residence in the tax year in which the transferee's status changes. The Revenue were successful before the courts in withholding the concession where they considered that it had been exploited for tax avoidance purposes: *R v IRC, ex p Fulford-Dobson* [1987] STC 344.

Income arising in the UK

6.8 It has been explained, in **1.4**, that a non-UK resident is subject to income tax on income from sources within the UK. An individual ceasing to be UK resident will therefore continue – in principle – to be taxable on any UK income which he had before leaving the UK. The scope for minimising the UK tax therefore depends in part upon the expatriate's ability to remove such sources from the UK, by transferring funds abroad. There are also specific exemptions which are available and the possibility of relief under a double taxation agreement.

UK pensions

6.9 A pension payable by a former employer will continue to be taxable in the hands of the expatriate if it is payable in the UK. This is so in the case of voluntary pensions: TA 1988 s 133(1), as well as pensions under approved occupational pension schemes: TA 1988 s 597(1). A pension payable under a personal pension scheme is chargeable to tax under Schedule E: TA 1988 s 19(1) para 4, and is treated as earned income of the recipient: TA 1988 s 643(3). There are exemptions for pensions paid under the following schemes:

(a) India, Pakistan, Burma and Colonial schemes;
(b) Pension funds for former public service employees of overseas territories;
(c) The Central African Pension Fund;
(d) The Overseas Service Pension Fund: TA 1988 s 615;
(e) Pension funds set up for overseas employees of UK employers: TA 1988 s 614.

6.10 In other cases, exemption from UK tax may be available under the terms of a double tax treaty. Commonly, taxing rights over pensions are reserved to the country of which the pensioner is a resident. Pensions paid out of public funds in the UK, however, are normally taxable in the UK – this would include national insurance retirement pension and pensions paid to former servants of the Crown. It is understood that national insurance retirement pensions payable to non-residents are regarded by the Revenue as falling within Extra-statutory concession B13 (see **6.32**). Such pensions may in any event be exempted from UK tax under tax treaty provisions if the pensioner is a national of the other country. As always, the particular tax treaty concerned must be consulted in each case to ascertain the position.

6.11 Generally speaking, there is little that can be done by the expatriate to remove a pension from the UK tax net. For individuals moving abroad on retirement, the simplest method of minimising UK income tax may be to elect to take the maximum tax-free lump sum available under the rules of the pension scheme, thereby commuting part of the pension that would otherwise be payable.

UK dividends

6.12 Dividends from UK companies carry a tax credit in the hands of UK residents (see **1.44**). UK dividends received by non-residents do not normally qualify for a tax credit. The 'net' dividend is treated as taxable income, without any addition for tax credit. However, a liability does not arise where the non-resident is subject only to the basic rate of income tax, because there is a credit for the notional amount of basic rate income tax on the 'net' dividend. If the non-resident is a resident of another country with which the UK has a double taxation agreement, it is often possible to claim a refund of the tax credit. Typically, the full tax credit is refunded, less a tax of 15% of the aggregate of dividend plus tax credit.

EXAMPLE

6.13 The position may be illustrated as follows:

	UK resident	Non-resident Normal	Non-resident Tax treaty
Dividend	75	75	75
Tax credit	25	–	25
Taxable income	100	75	100
Income tax	25*	–	15
Net receipt	75	75	85

*Assuming liability only at the basic rate.

6.14 Non-residents entitled to refund of tax credit under a UK double taxation agreement may be able to obtain the refund at source. The Revenue may authorise such arrangements where the non-resident's shares in the UK company are held through an approved nominee, and the UK company agrees. All shareholdings held by the nominee subject to the arrangement have to be designated as such in the company's share register. The refund of 15% of the 'gross' dividend, or 2/15ths of the dividend paid, is made by the company to the nominee. This procedure is usually referred to as the 'G' Arrangement: Double Taxation Relief (Taxes on Income) (General) (Dividend) Regulations 1973 SI 1973/317. Companies participating in the arrangement are noted in the Stock Exchange Daily Official List.

6.15 Certain non-residents are entitled to claim personal allowances which may result in a repayment of the tax credit: TA 1988 s 278 (see **1.24**). However the making of a personal allowances claim by a non-resident itself entitles the claimant to a tax credit in respect of the dividend: TA 1988 s 232(1). The effect of obtaining a tax credit depends upon the residence status of the individual. If he is resident in a country having a double tax treaty with the UK, the restriction of UK tax under the treaty may give a lower tax liability, in which case the provisions of the treaty should prevail.

EXAMPLE

6.16 GH, who is unmarried and is a British subject, has UK income of £20,000 in 1991/92, consisting wholly of UK dividends. He claims personal allowances under TA 1988 s 278.

(a) If GH cannot claim relief under a double taxation treaty, the position is as follows:

UK dividend	£20,000
Tax credit (25/75)	6,667
Gross income	26,667
Personal allowance	3,295
Taxable income	£23,372
Income tax on £23,372	£ 5,843.00
Tax credit	6,666.67
Tax repayable	£ 823.67

(b) If GH is a resident of the Netherlands, he is entitled to a tax credit but his UK income tax liability is restricted to 15% of the dividend plus the tax credit.

UK dividends	£20,000
Tax credit	6,667
Taxable income	£26,667
Tax at 15%	£ 4,000.00
Tax credit	6,666.67
Amount repayable	£ 2,666.67

In this case, the benefit of a personal allowances claim is displaced by the greater benefit available under the provisions of the UK/Netherlands tax treaty. A personal allowances claim might be of benefit if GH also had other UK source income, such as property rents, which do not attract any relief under the treaty.

Life assurance premiums

6.17   Relief for premiums paid on UK life policies issued before 14 March 1984 is given by deduction at source, so that only the net amount is paid over to the life office. On becoming non-resident, an individual normally ceases to be entitled to this tax relief and the premiums must be paid gross (but see **1.32** for exceptions). Nevertheless, by concession, the Revenue permit premiums to be paid net for the remainder of the tax year in which the individual becomes non-resident. Net payments may be resumed if the individual becomes resident again. Policies issued or varied after 13 March 1984 do not qualify for premium relief; TA 1988 s 266(3)(c).

UK real property

6.18   Income derived from the letting of real estate in the UK is taxable in broadly the same way as for UK residents. Property which is let unfurnished is taxable under Schedule A; and property which is let furnished is taxed under Schedule D Case VI: TA 1988 s 15. Allowable expenses from rental income include (TA 1988 s 25):

(1) agents' fees;
(2) accountancy fees;
(3) ground rents, etc;
(4) water rates, where borne by the landlord out of an inclusive rent;
(5) insurance premiums to insure the building and contents;
(6) repairs, redecoration and maintenance but not capital expenditure such as extensions, installation of central heating or double glazing;
(7) valuation fees;
(8) (for furnished lettings) wear and tear allowance of furniture. The amount given is 10% of the gross rent less water rates: Inland Revenue Press Release 13 October 1977.

In addition, capital allowances are available, at the taxpayer's option, for plant or machinery used for maintaining, repairing or managing the property: TA 1988 s 32.

6.19 Interest is not an allowable expense in computing net property rental income but may be given as a deduction from such income. The interest must be in respect of a loan to acquire or improve property, provided that it is let commercially for at least 26 weeks in any 52-week period, and either available for letting or under repair for the remainder of that period: TA 1988 s 355(1)(*b*). Any surplus of interest over net rental income may be offset against other UK rental income and any balance is then carried forward to the next year: TA 1988 s 355(4).

6.20 To qualify for relief, interest must:

(a) be paid on an advance from a bank carrying on bona fide banking business in the UK; or
(b) be UK source income (under Schedule D Case III) in the hands of the lender: TA 1988 s 353(1).

This is of particular importance to expatriates, who may purchase a UK property before their return, which is let in the meantime. If interest is to be offset against income for letting the property, the purchase price should not be borrowed offshore. Overdraft interest is never deductible, regardless of the source of the advance. Interest deductible from rents in respect of a let property is not within the MIRAS arrangements: TA 1988 s 370(6)(*b*), (7)(*a*).

6.21 Expatriates letting UK property as holiday accommodation may qualify for somewhat more advantageous tax treatment, in that the letting is treated as a trade: TA 1988 s 503. The main benefits for non-residents are that losses may be off set against other UK taxable income, and tax is payable in two instalments. However, the tax withholding requirement explained in **6.30** is not relaxed. The qualifying conditions are:

(a) the accommodation must be let furnished;

(b) the accommodation must be available for commercial letting to the public for at least 140 days;
(c) the actual lettings must amount to at least 70 days;
(d) no single let must exceed 31 days in any seven-month period which includes the minimum let periods as in (c).

The reference period for determining whether the property is let as holiday accommodation is normally the tax year.

Letting the private residence

6.22   An expatriate who lets his UK private residence whilst abroad will be taxed on the net rental income, as explained above. If the letting begins part way through the tax year, the property expenses for the year will need to be apportioned. This is done primarily by allocating to the rental period expenses which became due and were paid in that period. However, any cost of repairs of maintenance in respect of dilapidations attributable to the period of owner-occupation should be excluded: TA 1988 s 25(3)(*b*). In practice, the Revenue do not disallow routine maintenance costs, such as the costs of external repainting, which arise after the letting commenced. However, the costs of refurbishment carried out to facilitate letting following a period of owner-occupation might well be disallowed.

6.23   Interest on any loans to acquire or improve the property must also be apportioned according to the date of payment. The interest paid during the period of owner-occupation is deductible from income generally, while that paid after the individual becomes non-resident can be offset only against rental income, as described in **6.19**. Mortgage interest on a let property is also outside the rules for deduction of tax at source (MIRAS) and will normally have to be paid gross. There is an exception where the property was formerly the main residence and the expatriate claims the benefit of Extra-statutory concession A27 (see **6.26**). Strictly speaking, relief cannot be claimed for interest both under MIRAS and by deduction from letting income, but in practice the Revenue allow offset against rents even where A27 applies, with an appropriate adjustment for the basic rate relief given under MIRAS. The mere fact that the payer is non-resident does not take interest out of the MIRAS scheme.

6.24   A point to note for those with larger mortgages is that the £30,000 limit for interest relief does not apply when the interest is deductible against letting income from the property. Moreover, relief is not restricted to the basic rate of income tax only as in the case of owner-occupied properties. The amount of tax relief for mortgage interest could therefore rise as a result of leaving the UK, although admittedly it is then deductible only against UK property income.

6.25   The MIRAS (Mortgage Interest Relief At Source) system of tax relief on mortgage interest paid works by allowing the payer to make the interest payments to qualifying lenders net of basic rate income tax. Most bank, life company or building society mortgages will qualify. Tax relief at the higher rate (prior to 1991/92) is given by set-off in tax assessments. The property must be used as the only or main residence of the borrower: TA 1988 s 370(2)(*c*), or for certain pre-6 April 1988 loans, the main residence of the borrower's dependent relative, or of a former or separated spouse: FA 1988 s 44. The interest must be paid in the UK: TA 1988 s 370(1).

6.26 An expatriate living overseas may not be able to fulfil the only or main residence requirement especially where the UK property is no longer occupied by his family. There is an extra-statutory concession which allows absences of up to a year to be ignored for these purposes: Extra-statutory concession A27.

6.27 The concession also grants relief where a person is required to move to another location either in the UK or abroad, by reason of his employment, for a period of four years or less, he is entitled to tax relief on payments of interest on a mortgage which was to purchase a property as his principal private residence before his departure, provided the property can reasonably be expected to be his only or main residence on his return. The maximum period of relief is four years but if the property is reoccupied for a minimum of three months the four-year test will again be effective: IR Press Release 16 July 1976.

6.28 If an expatriate is working overseas and purchases a property in the UK during a period of leave, he will also be treated as satisfying the condition that the property was being used as his only or main residence before he went away, provided he uses the property as his only or main residence for a minimum of three months before he returns to his overseas employment.

6.29 When the property is let at a commercial rent the benefit of the concession may be claimed if this is more advantageous than a claim for relief against rental income.

Tax withholding

6.30 Where rent in respect of UK property is paid to a person whose 'usual place of abode' is outside the UK, the tenant must withhold income tax at the basic rate from the gross rental, and account to the Revenue for the tax withheld: TA 1988 s 43. The expression 'usual place of abode' is not defined for this purpose, although for other tax purposes it is defined as the country in which a person normally lives: TA 1988 s 195(9). Thus, it might be possible to avoid the withholding if non-residence resulted from a purely temporary absence from the UK eg for a period of two years. The withholding can also be avoided where the expatriate employee letting his UK property, appoints an agent who will receive the rent in the UK and on whom assessments may be made in the name of the non-resident: TMA 1970 s 78. In that case the tenant may pay the rent gross. When an agent is appointed, he becomes liable for any income tax liability and in practice he will require the lessor to indemnify him. The agent should prepare accounts to include all rents received and expenses incurred. After the deduction of expenses, the tax liability is then calculated on the net amount. This should avoid the basic rate income tax withholding before the rent is credited to the expatriate's account. It is worth noting that the withholding arrangements apply even if the lessee is also non-resident, although practically speaking it would be difficult to enforce, especially where payment is made outside the UK.

Gilt-edged stock

6.31   Where an individual is not ordinarily resident in the UK, income he receives from certain British Government Securities is exempt from UK tax (see Appendix 1): TA 1988 s 47. No new stocks carrying this exemption are now being issued but earlier exempt issues are still available. As most of these stocks have tax withheld at source, the non-ordinarily resident holder must apply for payment to be made to him gross. This application should be sent to the Inspector of Foreign Dividends although, in practice, the formalities are handled by the UK bank or stockbroker through which the stocks are purchased. Interest on 3½% War Loan, and on stocks and bonds held on the National Savings Bank Register, is normally paid gross. Holding exempt stocks on the NSB Register therefore avoids the need for exemption applications, although dealings are less flexible since postal instructions are required from the investor and there is a daily limit on dealings of £10,000 nominal value.

Bank deposit interest

6.32   Deposit accounts with UK banks can also be a useful investment for non-residents, depending upon the current yield. Although bank interest is not tax exempt for non-residents, it is not in practice assessed on them by the Revenue (Extra-statutory concession B13). The tax liability is enforced only where the non-resident claims tax relief on other income – for example, by way of a claim to personal allowances (see **1.24**). It is essential to note that the concession applies only where the individual is non-UK resident *throughout* the tax year. An expatriate who ceases to be UK resident part way through the year will still be assessable for that year on bank deposit interest. If a joint UK bank account is held by a couple where one spouse is resident and the other spouse is non-resident, the interest arising on the account is wholly taxable because the interest accrues to them jointly.

6.33   From 1991/92, UK bank interest is paid under deduction of tax at source: TA 1988 s 480A. A credit for income tax at the basic rate attaches to such interest and is refundable if the individual is liable at less than the basic rate. The tax liability of non-residents may be reduced under the provisions of double taxation agreements, in which case a refund may be claimed or authority sought for the bank to pay the interest subject to a reduced rate of withholding. In addition, interest may be paid gross on deposit accounts held, inter alia, by individuals not ordinarily resident in the UK who notify banks of their status: TA 1988 s 481(5)(*j*). There is also a requirement to advise the bank should the individual subsequently become UK ordinarily resident. Before 6 April 1991, the tax credit attaching to bank interest was not refundable.

6.34 It may be preferable to open a deposit account with an offshore branch or subsidiary of a British bank during a period of non-residence. This avoids the need to make an appropriate declaration to the bank and can avoid a UK tax liability where the concession referred to does not apply or the tax is recoverable by set-off resulting from a claim.

Building society interest

6.35 UK building societies pay interest net of tax. A person receiving this interest is treated as receiving it net of the basic rate of income tax. The tax credit on building society interest is, from 1991/92 onwards, repayable if the recipient is liable to income tax at less than the basic rate. As in the case of banks and other deposit takers, building societies may pay interest gross to individuals not ordinarily resident in the UK: IT (Building Societies) Regulations 1986 SI 1986/482, reg 6(1)(*a*).

Other interest

6.36 Where interest arising in the UK remains taxable in the hands of the non-resident, the basis of assessment is the amount arising in the preceding tax year if the interest is paid gross: TA 1988 s 64. There are special rules for new sources of interest, and for the cessation of a source, analogous to those applying to foreign income (see **4.6**). For interest paid net of tax, the assessment (to higher rates of tax only) is on a current year basis. The mere fact of becoming non-resident does not have any effect upon the basis of assessment. Interest from a continuing source will therefore be taxable for the first year of non-residence on the amount arising in the preceding year when the individual was resident, notwithstanding that residence changes during the current year.

Trust income

6.37 Income arising under a UK trust may or may not continue to be taxable in the UK. An annuity payable under a UK settlement will be subject to withholding at source by the trustees, at the basic rate of income tax. The rate of withholding is not normally reduced under treaty provisions but a refund may be claimed if, as is common, the treaty provides for the income to be taxed only in the country where the annuitant resides. For other trust income to which the non-resident is entitled, the tax treatment will depend upon the source of the underlying income receivable by the trustees. If the income arises from sources within the UK, it will be taxable in the UK, subject to any exemptions or to such relief as may be appropriate under a tax treaty, depending on the nature of the income. Foreign source income received by the trustees will not be subject to UK tax, notwithstanding that they may be UK resident: *Williams v Singer* [1921] 1 AC 65, 7 TC 387, HL. If UK resident trustees accumulate income for the benefit of a non-resident, or if a non-resident is a mere discretionary beneficiary, the trustees are taxed on the income at the rate equal to the sum of the basic rate and the additional rate of income tax: TA 1988 s 686. This applies also to UK source income accumulated by non-UK resident trustees: *IRC v Regent Trust Co Ltd* [1980] STC 140, [1980] 1 WLR 688.

Alimony and maintenance payments

6.38 Alimony payments receivable by a non-resident individual from a former spouse are not subject to income tax even if the payment is made under a UK court order: TA 1988 s 347(1)(*b*). There is an exception in the case of payments under a UK court order or deed made before 15 March 1988, although in this case the amount of taxable income is limited to the amount for 1988/89: FA 1988 s 38(4). In the case of payments made to a former or separated spouse who has not remarried, there is an alternative limitation of the amount of the married man's allowance for the year: FA 1988 s 38(5). Even if a maintenance payment is taxable, there is no withholding of income tax at source: FA 1988 s 38(7). The non-resident recipient, if taxable, may be entitled to exemption under a tax treaty.

6.39 Alimony payable under a foreign court order is not subject to withholding of UK income tax even where the payer is UK resident: *Keiner v Keiner* [1952] 1 All ER 643, 34 TC 346. The payments do not constitute UK source income in the hands of the recipient and, conversely, are not tax deductible for the payer: *Bingham v IRC* [1955] 3 All ER 321, 36 TC 254.

Overseas income

6.40 A non-UK resident is not subject to UK income tax on income arising outside the UK. This is so whether or not the income is remitted to the UK. It is therefore possible for an expatriate to remit such funds to the UK from abroad, to invest in the UK or to meet UK expenses, without tax liability. Where foreign income is received in the UK through a UK paying or collecting agent, a claim may be made for the tax withholding referred to in **4.23** not to apply. The non-resident must claim exemption by applying to the Inspector of Foreign Dividends: TA 1988 s 123(4). Proof of non residence is required in the form of a declaration or affidavit. The Revenue do not grant exemption if the dividends etc arise in respect of shares or securities held in bearer form.

6.41 The basis of assessment of income does not change merely because the individual's residence status changes (see **8.11**). Consequently, for a continuing source, the normal preceding year basis would apply, so that for the year of departure the individual would be assessed on the income arising in the preceding year. In practice, the Revenue limit any assessment to the smaller of

(a) the proportion of the assessable income that the period 6 April to the date of departure bears to the whole tax year in which the individual leaves the UK;
(b) the amount of income actually arising in the period from 6 April to the date of departure: IR20 para 76.

In the case of non-UK domiciled individuals, the amount of income actually remitted to the UK in the period from 6 April to the date of departure is substituted for the amount arising in (b). Thus it is beneficial for non-UK domiciliaries to remit no overseas income to the UK in the year of departure. This practice does not apply to income arising in the Irish Republic. For income received through a UK paying or collecting agent, the amount so received after ceasing to be UK resident is not taxable and exemption may be claimed (see **6.40**): IR20 para 76.

EXAMPLE

6.42 BM is domiciled in the UK and owns shares in a US company, which he bought in 1985. On 30 September 1991, he leaves the UK for permanent residence abroad. Dividends are paid on the shares as follows:

16 April 1990	£2,250
4 November 1990	3,400
30 April 1991	2,700
5 November 1991	3,200

The income assessable under Schedule D Case V for 1991/92 is £5,650 ie on the preceding year basis. Under the Revenue concession, the assessment is restricted to the smaller of:

(a) $6/12 \times £5,650 = £2,825$
(b) The amount arising in the period 6 April to 30 September 1991 ie £2,700

The assessment for 1991/92 is therefore £2,700.

6.43 Where an individual who is a resident of the UK receives certain types of income from a country which has a double taxation agreement with the UK, he may be entitled to exemption from foreign tax, or a reduction of the rate of withholding tax. By ceasing to be a UK resident the individual is no longer entitled to protection under UK tax treaties and may therefore suffer higher foreign withholding taxes. The position will depend upon the individual's tax status in the country of residence and the existence or otherwise of appropriate double taxation agreements entered into by that country.

Capital gains

6.44 An individual who is neither resident nor ordinarily resident is not subject to CGT, whether or not the assets are situated in the UK: CGTA 1979 s 2, except for

(a) UK branch assets: CGTA 1979 s 12;
(b) certain offshore oil and gas assets: FA 1973 s 38 (see **1.5**).

Chargeable gains realised in the tax year on or prior to the date of departure are subject to CGT, but gains realised subsequently are not: IR20 para 74. However, an individual who is not leaving the UK for employment overseas needs to consider carefully the risk that he will not remain outside the UK for a full 36 months and hence that UK ordinary residence will not cease immediately after the date of departure.

6.45 In these circumstances, the individual should at least ensure that there is one complete tax year in which his home is abroad and during which he does not set foot in the UK. Disposals of assets should then be made in that year. There is a considerable risk that disposals made in the tax year of departure, after the date of departure, will still be subject to CGT. In a case where a married woman transferred an asset to her husband who was about to depart overseas for employment, the Revenue withheld their concession in relation to the disposal of the asset after the husband had left the UK: *R v IRC, ex p Fulford-Dobson* [1987] STC 344. The position may be affected if the individual is resident, at the time of the disposal, in a country having a double taxation agreement with the UK which limits UK tax on capital gains.

Gifts rollover

6.46 Although there is no general CGT charge on becoming non-resident, there may be a recapture in some circumstances. If an individual has received a gift while resident in the UK, and the donor's chargeable gain has, by election, been rolled over against the donee's base cost, the rolled-over gain (but not any subsequent gain) crystallises if the donee ceases to be UK resident within six years of the gift: FA 1981 s 79(1),(2),(6). This 'exit charge' does not apply if emigration is for the purposes of working abroad and residence is resumed within three years, without the asset having been disposed of in the interim: FA 1981 s 79(5). The expatriate cannot rely on defeating any recapture by being outside of the jurisdiction, since the Revenue have recourse to the original donor if the CGT is not paid within 12 months: FA 1981 s 79(7).

Spouse remaining resident

6.47 If the expatriate's wife or husband remains in the UK, the CGT position is broadly the same as if they had both remained resident, provided that they are still treated as living together, in the income tax sense: *Gubay v Kington* [1984] 1 All ER 513, [1984] STC 99, HL. Transfers can therefore be made by the resident spouse to the non-resident spouse, who may subsequently dispose of the asset free of CGT. However, any attempts to structure a pre-arranged sale to a third party in this way are likely to be nullified, following the courts' present thinking on such transactions: *Furniss v Dawson* [1984] AC 474, [1984] STC 153, HL. The Revenue withheld their concessionary treatment where a similar arrangement was adopted but the asset was sold in the year in which the transferee spouse went abroad, after the date of departure: *R v IRC, ex p Fulford-Dobson* [1987] STC 344.

Private residence exemption

6.48   Absence abroad can have an effect upon the exemption available for capital gains on disposal of a private residence. The detailed considerations are explained in chapter 7.

Capital tax planning

6.49   Change of residence status is unlikely to have any effect upon IHT liability except in two types of case. First, as the incidence of IHT depends primarily on domicile, an individual leaving the UK to take up permanent residence abroad may be able to acquire a new domicile by virtue of the move (see **3.6**). Gifts or bequests of property would then attract IHT only if the property were located in the UK. As indicated in the discussion of domicile, the answer in any particular case will depend upon a number of factors in addition to the change of residence. It should also be noted that an individual domiciled in the UK retains UK domicile for IHT purposes for three years after acquiring a new domicile elsewhere (see **3.15**).

6.50   A residence change can also have a direct effect upon domicile where an individual is not domiciled in the UK in general law but has resided here for many years. For IHT, an individual is deemed to be domiciled in the UK if he has been resident for 17 or more years out of the last 20 (see **3.16**). As the limit is being approached it may – depending upon the circumstances – benefit an individual to become non-resident for a year or two in order to postpone becoming UK domiciled. This would enable gifts or settlements involving foreign property to be made without IHT liability.

Foreign tax implications

6.51   UK residents working or moving abroad will almost always come within the jurisdiction of foreign taxing authorities. The burden of foreign income taxes is in many cases equal to or greater than that of UK income tax. There is therefore little point making elaborate arrangements to minimise UK tax liability if as a result it is merely replaced by an equivalent or greater tax liability elsewhere. The implications of foreign residence are discussed in **2.22**.

6.52   A particular point to watch is that the foreign country may have different rules from the UK regarding tax deductions. For example, interest payments on a mortgage in the UK may not be deductible for income tax in the country concerned. Although the individual may often be able to deduct the interest in the UK if he is letting the property, there will often be no tax relief at all if he cannot. UK pension scheme contributions may also become more costly for individuals who move abroad, because many countries do not recognise foreign pension schemes and disallow any contributions to them. Life assurance premiums paid to UK life offices may similarly be non-deductible abroad. This is of particular relevance for individuals who are not resident in the UK and obtain no UK tax relief on the premiums.

Social security

6.53   For individuals going abroad for lengthy periods, liability to pay UK national insurance contributions will usually cease. Where the expatriate intends to return, there may be some benefit in making voluntary (Class 3) contributions, although these count only towards long-term national insurance benefits such as retirement and widow's pensions. It may well be that foreign social security contributions are payable whilst abroad and these may be creditable against the individual's UK contributions record. The social security implications of overseas employments are considered in chapter 7.

UK benefits available abroad

6.54   Generally speaking, entitlement to social security UK benefits is affected by absence abroad. Some benefits can be paid abroad only in certain circumstances and there are restrictions on entitlement to benefits as a result of events, such as accidents at work, that happen while working outside the UK. The following table indicates the position on the main UK benefits:

Benefit	*Comment*
Retirement pension Widow's benefits	Payable anywhere abroad
Sickness benefit Maternity benefits	Payable in EC countries or under reciprocal agreement
Unemployment benefit	Payable only in EC countries
Industrial injuries benefits	Payable under EC regulations or reciprocal agreements
Child benefit	Payable in EC countries; otherwise, only for absence of up to 6 months

6.55   Medical treatment under the NHS is available only in the UK and no reimbursement of foreign medical costs is made under the scheme. However, there are reciprocal health care arrangements with a number of countries whereby medical services may be obtained free or at a reduced cost. Not all of these countries are ones with which there is a bilateral social security agreement. The type of health care available varies from country to country and it is essential to check in advance what kind of treatment can be obtained. Even where public health services are available, it may be advisable to take out private medical cover before leaving the UK.

Visas and work permits

6.56 It is impossible to generalise about visa requirements since these will vary from country to country. For EC countries, entry visas and work permits are not required by UK citizens, but some countries require registration by non-nationals with the local police authorities. Individuals who are not British citizens should check carefully before leaving the UK that they retain the right of re-entry to the UK on their return.

7 Overseas employees

7.1 Employees who lose their UK resident status as a result of an extended tour of duty outside the UK will be largely in the same tax position as other long-term expatriates, as explained in chapter 6. The conditions under which UK residence ceases following departure from the UK are set out in **2.14**. In this chapter, special considerations likely to be of application to expatriate employees are considered, with special reference to the tax implications of returning to the UK.

7.2 The chief disadvantage that may arise on becoming non-resident is that the 100% deduction for longer absences cannot be claimed (see **5.28**). If the individual continues to perform UK duties, which are not disregarded on the grounds that they are incidental to the performance of overseas duties, a UK tax liability could arise under Schedule E Case II. It might be preferable in these circumstances to continue to be UK resident, provided that the conditions for claiming the 100% deduction can be satisfied (see **5.28**). Alternatively, it might be possible to claim exemption from UK tax under the terms of a double taxation agreement.

Residence rulings

7.3 At the date of departure, it is not possible to be certain that the requisite conditions will be fulfilled. The Revenue normally therefore give a provisional ruling that the individual has ceased to be resident and ordinarily resident in the UK from the date following the date of departure. The position is reviewed at the end of the first full tax year following the year of departure. The provisional ruling will permit the UK employer to exclude the employee's earnings from tax withholding under the PAYE scheme. However, it is prudent to make some provision for tax that might become due where the likelihood of satisfying the conditions is doubtful.

7.4 Prior to departure from the UK, the employee should file form P85 with the tax office handling his tax affairs. Form P85 is a questionnaire intended to provide the Revenue with sufficient information to make a residence ruling. Adequate time should be allowed for obtaining a ruling, bearing in mind that files are invariably submitted by the local tax office to Claims Branch (Foreign Division). Form P85 incorporates a claim to repayment of tax which may be refundable as a result of the employee's departure (see **6.4**). Where the employee is terminating his contract in order to take up a new employment, the form P45 which he receives from his old employer should accompany the refund claim. Where the UK employment continues, the Revenue will issue PAYE code 'NT' to the employer to enable salary to be paid gross.

Employment income

7.5 Earnings for duties performed outside the UK are not subject to income tax if the employee is not resident in the UK. Even where there are UK duties, they are treated as performed abroad if they are merely incidental to the performance of non-UK duties: TA 1988 s 132(2) (see **2.10** as to the meaning of 'incidental'). Earnings for UK duties not falling under this heading will be taxable under Schedule E Case II, and an apportionment of total remuneration is required where there is no separate contract for the UK duties. In general, the Revenue will accept an apportionment based upon the number of working days spent in the UK and abroad respectively: Statement of Practice SP5/84.

Payment in the UK

7.6 The remittance to the UK of overseas earnings has no tax effect if the employee is non-resident. It therefore makes no difference to his UK tax liability if all or part of his remuneration is credited to his bank account in the UK.

7.7 Foreign exchange controls often constitute a factor in deciding where an expatriate employee's earnings are paid to him. If paid locally, salary may not be freely remittable and it may help avoid this problem if at least part of it is paid in the UK. The existence of continuing financial commitments in the UK, and the possible exchange exposure on earnings paid in some foreign currencies, also point to the wisdom of receiving salary in the UK. There may sometimes be a resulting reduction in local taxes if part of the earnings are received outside that country, although this arrangement cannot be recommended if it relics merely on non-disclosure for its effectiveness. Tax authorities everywhere are increasingly imposing tax on the full amount of expatriate workers' earnings and each case must be checked to ensure that any arrangement does not involve contravention of foreign tax laws.

Expenses and benefits

7.8 Any amounts that would normally have been included in taxable remuneration had the employee remained UK resident should be treated in the same way as salary. Unless expenses and benefits are related exclusively to UK or foreign duties respectively, the correct treatment would appear to be to add them to cash remuneration and apportion the total as described in **7.5**. It is not possible to avoid the benefit taxation rules even where the amount of UK remuneration is less than £8,500, since this figure is expressed to be an annual rate without distinguishing between taxable and non-taxable elements: TA 1988 s 167(1)(*b*).

7.9 Consequently, if expenses are paid in respect of a non-resident employee's visits to the UK to perform UK duties, they will be taxable subject to a deduction for expenses necessarily incurred (see **5.11**). Similarly, a car or accommodation provided in the UK are likely to be regarded as taxable benefits to be added to the amount taxable under Case II, although it might in some circumstances be possible to exclude a proportion of the benefit if it relates to an overall service contract encompassing non-UK as well as UK duties. Expenses and benefits purely in respect of overseas duties will not be taxable.

7.10 Where an employee is required by his employer to change his residence for the purpose of working in another location, costs of relocation met or reimbursed by the employer are by concession exempt from income tax if they are reasonable in amount and payment is properly controlled: Extra-statutory Concession A5. The concession does not distinguish between a relocation within the UK and a relocation abroad and thus an employee moving overseas for work purposes should be able to obtain exemption. In practice, the scope of the concession is a matter of negotiation in the light of the particular circumstances. The Revenue seem unwilling to grant the concession where the old residence is not sold, which may pose a particular difficulty in the case of overseas relocations which are not permanent. As well as the costs of removal of household effects, and the incidental costs of buying a new house and selling the old one, the concession may extend to the reimbursement of other expenses occasioned directly by the relocation. There is a general restriction on betterment, so that payments for furnishings etc are tax-free only to the extent that they enable the employer to replace items with those of equivalent quality and type. A general disturbance allowance may be exempted, in addition to specific expenses, although in practice the Revenue are unlikely to agree amounts which are materially in excess of £2,000.

UK pension scheme membership

7.11 Employees of UK resident employers will often be members of an occupational pension scheme under which the employee and/or the employer contributes. Contributions by the employer are tax deductible and are not treated as taxable benefits to the employee where the pension scheme has been approved by the Inland Revenue under statutory powers. Employees' contributions to approved schemes are also tax deductible against their earnings.

7.12 The conditions for approval are detailed and are set out in a booklet IR12 issued by the Inland Revenue Superannuation Funds Office. The general conditions as to benefits provided, trustee arrangements and so forth are outside the scope of this work but is is necessary to be aware of the rules relating to overseas service by pension scheme members.

7.13 Basically, all employees who are members of an approved UK pension scheme remain within that scheme regardless of where their duties are performed, or whether or not they are resident in the UK: IR12 para 17.7. Thus, even if the employee is non-resident or his earnings attract the 100% deduction, superannuation contributions may still be paid into the scheme and service will count towards retirement benefits.

7.14 The main tax problem that arises where the employee is not liable to UK tax on his earnings is that, if foreign tax is payable, UK pension scheme contributions are often not tax deductible in the other country. In addition, contributions by the employer may be taxable benefits in that country. The position will need to be checked in each case.

Non-resident employer

7.15 Where it is necessary for commercial or organisational reasons that the employee is employed abroad by a non-resident firm or company, difficulties can arise in relation to membership of the UK pension scheme. However, a non-resident employer can participate in the UK pension scheme provided that:

(a) the UK employer and the overseas employer are sufficiently closely associated. For companies, a 51% subsidiary relationship would be adequate;
(b) the employee remains 'effectively chargeable' to income tax on his earnings. This means that he must remain resident in the UK, his earnings must not attract the 100% deduction nor must they be taxable on the remittance basis.
(IR12 para 17.8)

7.16 Contributions to the UK scheme by the foreign employer will not necessarily be tax deductible at the corporate level, and the position should be checked in each case.

7.17 If some or all of the overseas employees do not satisfy the second condition in **7.15**, the part of the scheme relating to those employees is deemed to be a separate, unapproved scheme which is not tax exempt. The Revenue then requires an actuarial valuation of the fund referable to each part of the scheme, and each item of income or gains has subsequently to be apportioned between the two.

Secondment

7.18 One way around the above difficulty is to second employees to overseas employers for a limited period. For periods of secondment of up to three years, Revenue approval is not required for the employees to remain in the UK pension scheme: IR12 para 3.9. The Revenue will also approve longer term engagements, for example, where the employee has a succession of overseas employments, if the UK employer at all times retains control over the movements of the employee. In either case, the overseas employer must reimburse the UK employer for the contributions paid. Again, there could be tax problems for the overseas employer.

7.19 If the employee moves abroad permanently his accrued benefits in the UK scheme are frozen, subject to any possible transfer value being payable to an overseas scheme.

Separate pension schemes

7.20 Alternatively, separate schemes may be set up for those working overseas. Where the employee is employed by an overseas employer, he may participate in a non-resident pension scheme, which does not require approval by the UK Revenue. Employees' contributions to the scheme will not be deductible for UK tax but that may not matter, as it is likely that either the remuneration will attract the 100% deduction or the employee will be non-resident.

7.21 If employees whose earnings are taxable are included in such a scheme, and so that approval needs to be sought, it will be given only if there is a UK resident agent for the pension fund administrator. However, periods during which remuneration is not 'effectively chargeable', as defined in **7.15**, cannot count as qualifying service for pension benefits.

7.22 The UK agent is required to pay all the pensions relating to UK resident pensioners and to subject them to PAYE. Although foreign pensions attract a 10% deduction for UK income tax: TA 1988 s 65(2), UK resident pensioners lose the 10% deduction when the pension is paid by the UK agent: IR12 para 17.4. The non-resident scheme is more appropriate for local staff and for UK expatriates who have gone abroad permanently and intend to retire overseas.

7.23 To avoid the difficulties of a partially approved scheme, a UK employer may set up a separate UK scheme for those working wholly overseas in connection with a trade or undertaking carried on wholly or partly outside the UK: TA 1988 s 615(3),(6). If the scheme is established under irrevocable trusts solely for the purpose of providing superannuation benefits to such employees and is recognised by employer and employees it will qualify for advantageous tax treatment in that:

(a) investment income arising to the trustees will be treated as income arising to an individual not resident, not ordinarily resident and not domiciled in the UK, so that foreign source income will effectively be tax exempt;
(b) gains on the disposal of assets by the trustees are exempt from capital gains tax.

There is no specific provision that employer contributions to such a scheme are tax deductible, in contrast to the position for UK approved schemes, and any claim to deduct any such contribution would need to be under the normal rules. Similarly, there is no general exclusion from tax for employees in respect of employer contributions, although tax is not charged where the employee's emoluments are not chargeable under Schedule E Case I or Case II: TA 1988 s 596(2)(*a*).

7.24 Under the type of scheme referred to in **7.23**, pensions paid to UK resident pensioners are not within Schedule E and consequently are subject to deduction of tax only at the basic rate, not under PAYE. Pensions paid to non-resident pensioners are not subject to income tax and are payable gross: TA 1988 s 615(3). These aspects could be beneficial, provided sufficient gross and taxed income is received to cover each type of pension. This type of scheme is also available to overseas employees and could be useful if it is desirable to have pensions paid in sterling rather than in a foreign currency. Where the employer is in a position to gain Revenue approval for a scheme, that will normally be preferable to a s 615 scheme, however.

7.25 For employees who have gone overseas to work in circumstances such that they cease to be UK resident, personal pension schemes are not generally available. This is because the annual contribution ceiling to a personal pension scheme is defined by reference to relevant earnings: TA 1988 s 638(3),(4). Relevant earnings are those which are chargeable to tax: TA 1988 s 644(1), and in the case of a non-resident would include only earnings for UK duties, within Schedule E Case II. If there are no UK duties, no contributions to a personal pension scheme are permitted. Nevertheless, plans to which contributions have previously been made may continue in existence and contributions may be resumed on the expatriate's return to the UK.

Stock option and incentive arrangements

7.26 Share options issued to employees are not normally taxable on issue but only on exercise, assignment or release: TA 1988 s 135. The treatment of options is unclear if the employee is non-UK resident when the option is exercised, whether or not he was resident at the time it was issued. The doubt arises because the tax charge on options is under Schedule E but not under any particular case of that Schedule: TA 1988 s 135(1). It might therefore be argued that gains from exercising share options were taxable if attributable to UK duties, emoluments for which would be within Schedule E Case II. It is understood that the Revenue may take the view that the gains are taxable regardless of attribution to UK duties, because the charge under Schedule E need not be under any specific Case. This is contrary to the view expressed in the Revenue booklet IR25: para 5.2 (now withdrawn).

7.27 The charge to income tax on share options does not apply unless they are issued when the employee is within Schedule E Case I, that is both resident and ordinarily resident in the UK: TA 1988 s 140(1). A period of non-residence because of an overseas tour of duty therefore enables options to be issued to the employee that will never be subject to income tax even if exercised after UK residence is resumed.

7.28 Tax benefits attach to membership of a savings related or other approved share option scheme. The rules are detailed and largely outside the scope of this work. If a member of such a scheme moves overseas to work whilst remaining in the employment of the scheme company or group, there is no immediate impact on scheme membership. There is no requirement as to residence nor as to emoluments being within Case I or Case II of Schedule E. However, in the case of an approved option scheme other than a savings related scheme, there is a ceiling on the value of shares to be acquired by the option holder. The ceiling is the greater of £100,000 of four times the employee's earnings subject to PAYE in either the current or the preceding tax year: TA 1988 Sch 9 para 28(2). If the employee is on a long term assignment overseas, so that his earnings are not chargeable to UK tax, the ceiling will effectively be £100,000.

7.29 The issue of shares to employees is taxable, the amount assessable being the difference between the market value of the shares and the amount, if any, the employee pays for them: *Weight v Salmon* (1935) 153 LT 55, 19 TC 174. If there are special restrictions attaching to the shares, then there will be a tax charge when they are removed or varied, but only if the value of the shares is thereby increased: TA 1988 s 78(2). The amount assessable is the increase in value resulting from the removal or variation of restrictions. A similar consequence follows if rights attaching to the shares are created or varied, if restrictions on other shares are created or varied, or rights attaching to other shares are removed or varied. Tax charges under Schedule E also arise if the shares concerned are shares in a dependent subsidiary ie one which has significant transactions with other companies in the same group, or if special benefits are received by the employee as a result of holding the shares.

7.30 As in the case of options, shares acquired in a share incentive scheme may be able to be disposed of by the employee without tax penalty if he ceases to be UK resident although the position is not free from doubt (see **7.25**). Incentive shares issued at a time when the employee is not resident or not ordinary resident in the UK are not within the scope of the income tax charge described above, because the charge applies only where shares are issued to an employee taxable under Schedule E Case I: FA 1988 s 77(2). There is however a further exposure for a higher paid employee or director acquiring shares at less than market value. The amount of the undervalue is deemed to be a loan to the employee or director and he then faces an annual tax charge on notional interest, and is taxed on the full amount of the 'loan' if the shares are sold: TA 1988 s 162. This provision is not affected by the employee's or director's residence status when the shares are issued, and thus would be a problem if he resumed UK residence without having disposed of the shares.

Termination payments

7.31 A termination payment made to a non-resident director or employee, whether by way of compensation for loss of office or otherwise, is in principle taxable, regardless of whether the individual may have performed

UK duties in the past: TA 1988 s 148. Such payments are taxable under Schedule E, without reference to a specific case. It is arguable that a non-resident employee cannot be assessed under Schedule E save under Case II, and this implies UK duties. However, there are express provisions exempting payments in respect of employments involving foreign service: TA 1988 s 188(3). This may weaken the argument relating generally to non-residents, because in the absence of such provisions it would appear that the payment would be taxable whether it related to UK or to foreign duties. Payments in respect of the employee's entering into a restrictive covenant (for example, not to compete with the employer for a certain period after leaving service) are taxable if the non-resident individual performed UK duties within Case II: TA 1988 s 313(1), (6) but not otherwise. The payment is taxable in full, and the £30,000 exemption applicable to termination payments is not available.

Overseas taxation

7.32   Non-UK resident employees and directors will often be subject to tax on their earnings in a country outside the UK, either because they are resident there or because their duties are carried out there. The tax rules vary from country to country. It will sometimes be found that some countries do not possess the sophisticated rules for taxing expenses and benefits that exist in the UK. It may therefore be possible to achieve tax savings by means of arrangements which have long since been nullified for UK tax purposes. Nevertheless, it should not be forgotten that the approach of many foreign tax jurisdictions to tax planning is different from that in the UK, and it is often based upon legal principles which permit the setting aside of 'artificial' transactions. Any proposed arrangements must always be checked very carefully with professional advisers in the country concerned.

Double taxation relief

7.33   Where an employee ceases to be resident in the UK he leaves behind the protection of UK double taxation agreements against tax in countries in which he may be working. If he takes up residence in another country, he can claim relief or exemption under that country's treaties, if any. In circumstances where he does not become a resident of another country – for example, where the overseas assignment involves travelling from one place to another without any fixed base – then the expatriate will not normally be eligible to claim relief under any double taxation agreement. This could involve double taxation and loss of tax allowances.

7.34   This type of assignment may be one instance where it could be preferable to retain UK residence and claim relief under UK treaties. UK personal allowances would also be available. Provided that the employment earnings qualified for the 100% deduction, there should be no UK tax cost, although remaining UK resident does eliminate the potential for tax-free investment outside the UK.

Investment opportunities

7.35 Individuals who are not resident in the UK are not taxable in the UK on income from investments abroad. As in the case of employment income for offshore duties, remittance of the income to the UK has no tax effect. Non-resident employees do have the opportunity while abroad to invest savings from their earnings, or indeed any capital, to achieve a yield which is free of UK tax. Local taxes and exchange controls often make it undesirable to invest in the country where the expatriate is working and off-shore financial centres may be a suitable home for investments. Never-theless, the attraction of tax-free investment should not obscure the fact that the incidental costs of using tax havens can be high. In particular, manage-ment charges of offshore funds are often heavier than in the UK and the terms of any investment always need careful scrutiny.

Offshore funds

7.36 An investment in an offshore fund may have advantages for the intending expatriate. The tax benefit is that interest rolls up in the fund and does not attract a tax liability until sold (see **4.44**). The individual can therefore plan to sell his investment during a year in which he is a non-resident of the UK. It is important to consider the realisation of such investments well in advance of the employee's permanent return to the UK.

Gilts

7.37 Expatriates who cease to be ordinarily resident in the UK may find exempt gilts (see **6.31**) a relatively flexible investment. Not only is the interest free of UK tax whilst they remain abroad, but there is no need to dispose of the stock before resuming UK residence, as it is not subject to CGT: CGTA 1979 s 67.

Capital transactions

7.38 Assuming that the individual ceases to be ordinarily resident in the UK, capital transactions may be carried out free of CGT. Where it is possible to do so without incurring significant incidental costs, assets could be sold and repurchased so at to obtain an uplift in base cost before the individual returns to the UK. However, assets standing at a loss should not be sold since the loss would not be allowable. Another aspect requiring consideration is the sale of assets previously gifted to the employee while in the UK, with the benefit of a rollover election (see **1.6**). Although there can be recapture of rolled-over gains when the employee becomes non-resident, this is not the case where he resumes UK residence within three years and has not disposed of the asset in the interim: FA 1981 s 79(5). Nevertheless, any gain accruing subsequent to the gift is not recaptured, and the tax saving in realising that gain outside the UK tax net could well outweigh the recaptured CGT on the earlier gift.

7.39 Expatriate employees who are considering changing their UK private residence on their return to the UK should plan such a move carefully, even in circumstances where the property has not been let. If the old property is not sold until after the expatriate resumes residence in the UK, a CGT liability could arise. There are various reliefs for absences abroad for employment, but the rules are complex and do not necessarily cover all situations.

7.40 When an individual disposes of a property which has been his principal private residence throughout his period of ownership, the gain arising on the sale is not a chargeable gain: CGTA 1979 s 102(1). If the property is disposed of while the individual is neither resident nor ordinarily resident in the UK, the question of exemption does not arise, since the gains are not subject to CGT: CGTA 1979 s 2(1).

7.41 Where a house has been used as the principal private residence for only part of the period of ownership, only part of the gain is exempt and must be apportioned: CGTA 1979 s 102(2). However, there are some periods of non-occupation which are, in effect, treated as periods of residence, as follows:

(a) any period up to 36 months following the end of owner-occupation is ignored: CGTA 1979 s 102(1);
(b) a concession also allows a 12-month period before occupation to be ignored if the house is being repaired or built or the sale of the prior residence has not been completed: Inland Revenue Press Release, 29 August 1972.

For disposals before 19 March 1991, the period allowed under (a) was 24 months, although the 24 month period may be reinstated at a later date by Treasury Order: CGTA 1979 s 102(5).

7.42 Other periods are also treated as being periods of residence if they are preceded and followed by periods of occupation and the property is the only one which is eligible for relief: CGTA 1979 s 102(3). These periods are:

(a) any period not exceeding three years;
(b) any period of employment wholly outside the UK;
(c) any period not exceeding four years where the absence results from the location of the workplace, or a condition of the employment.

All these categories may be cumulated, so that – for example – a period of absence for employment elsewhere in the UK could be for up to 7 years ((a) plus (c)). The most important of the above reliefs for the expatriate is (b), whereby any period of overseas employment is treated as a period of residence. If a person cannot resume occupation in his former residence because he is required to work in another location, the condition relating to resumption of residence is deemed to be satisfied: Extra-statutory concession D4.

7.43 One pitfall is the condition requiring re-occupation after the period of absence. If the property is not re-occupied simply because the expatriate has acquired a new home in the UK, and not for reasons connected with his employment, the period of absence will not be disregarded and a chargeable gain can arise. It is therefore important for the expatriate to allow sufficient time before his return to the UK for the old property to be sold.

7.44 Another point sometimes overlooked is that periods of absence are disregarded only if the individual had no other property eligible for the CGT relief. In practice, individuals often acquire an interest in an overseas property, if only by way of a monthly tenancy. In these circumstances, the Revenue seem to accept that the period of absence is to be disregarded provided that the individual elects for the UK property to be treated as the main private residence, under CGTA 1979 s 101(5). To be fully effective, the election should be made within two years of acquiring an interest in the second property.

7.45 Where a capital gain on disposal of a residence is only partially exempt, and it was let during the period of ownership, a further exemption is available for the period of letting. The let property exemption is £40,000 or, if less, the amount of the owner-occupier exemption due: FA 1980 s 80. The maximum exemption was £20,000 for disposals before 19 March 1991. This additional exemption applies to a letting of the whole or a part of the residence during the period of ownership.

Social security and benefits

7.46 Moving abroad to work may have an effect upon the liability to pay UK national insurance contributions. Although ceasing to be liable may apparently be a welcome relief, it should be remembered that any gap in contributions could affect benefit entitlement on returning to the UK. In addition, there may be a liability to pay foreign social security contributions. Even if creditable for UK benefit purposes, they are likely to be at a higher rate than national insurance contributions, while the individual is unlikely ever to be in a position to claim the correspondingly higher foreign benefits.

Working abroad for a UK employer

7.47 For employees going abroad to work for an employer having a place of business in the UK, the basic rule is that liability for UK contributions continues for the first 52 weeks of the overseas assignment. The employee must, however, be ordinarily resident in the UK and be resident immediately before leaving the UK. 'Ordinarily resident' is not defined but in practice the Department of Social Security (DSS) regard a person as remaining ordinarily resident if he returns to the UK within five years of departure, unless the intention to return is abandoned before the end of that period. For a more extended absence, a ruling should be sought from the DSS Overseas Branch.

7.48   Where there is no continuing liability to pay contributions for the first 52 weeks of absence, short-term benefits may normally be claimed on return to the UK as though contributions had been paid throughout, although voluntary contributions (see **7.49**) would have to be paid to preserve pension and widow's benefit entitlement.

Foreign employer

7.49   Where the employee goes abroad to work for a foreign employer, who has no place of business in the UK, liability to pay contributions ceases on taking up the new employment. This could be the case, for example, on a transfer within an international group of companies. It is possible to pay Class 3 voluntary contributions in these circumstances, but they count only for retirement pension and widow's benefits, not for unemployment, sickness and other short-term benefits.

Self-employed individuals

7.50   Self-employed persons are not liable for basic (Class 2) national insurance contributions for any week for which they are working outside the UK. However, Class 4 (profit-related) contributions continue to be payable unless the individual ceases to be UK resident for tax purposes.

Foreign social security payments

7.51   Most developed countries abroad impose a liability to social security contributions even on non-residents or temporary residents who work or live there. In many cases, the employer is liable to pay contributions although it may be difficult to enforce the liability if the employer is a UK resident with no assets or place of business in the other country.

7.52   As already mentioned, contribution rates abroad (especially in Europe) are often higher than in the UK, although this is usually reflected in more generous levels of social security benefit. Another difference from the UK is that foreign social security contributions are often tax deductible for the employee, which reduces their effective cost. Nevertheless, such contributions will not be tax deductible in the UK nor will they be credited against liability to pay UK national insurance contributions. Where an employee remains UK resident, therefore, any liability for foreign contributions can be penal, and it is expensive for the employer to make good the cost under a salary equalisation scheme.

Bilateral agreements

7.53 The UK has made a number of bilateral social security agreements with foreign countries. These agreements cover benefit entitlement and, in some cases, double liability to pay social security contributions. Special arrangements exist for EC countries and these are discussed below. Other countries with which reciprocal agreements have been made are as follows:

Australia*	Israel	Philippines
Austria	Jamaica	Sweden
Bermuda	Jersey and Guernsey	Switzerland
Canada*	Malta	Turkey
Cyprus	Mauritius	USA
Finland	New Zealand*	Yugoslavia
Iceland	Norway	

*Agreement covers benefits only

7.54 The precise terms of the agreements will vary from country to country. In particular it is essential to check that all elements of the foreign contributions are covered.

7.55 The agreements generally apply by reference to citizenship or nationality rather than residence. Many agreements concluded before 1983 refer to citizens of the United Kingdom and Colonies. From 1 January 1983, this category was abolished by the British Nationality Act 1981, and such agreements are now deemed to include British citizens, British Dependent Territories Citizens and British Overseas Citizens. Where an agreement covers contributions, not just benefits, there is provision for relief from social security contributions in the other country, subject to production of evidence from the DSS that liability continues under the UK scheme (see **7.47** above). Where the period spent in the other country exceeds 52 weeks, so that national insurance contributions are no longer payable, it is usually possible to continue to be exempt from foreign contributions provided prior application is made.

7.56 If the employer is resident in the other country then there is no exemption and full contributions are payable under the foreign scheme. However, the agreements normally provide that payment of foreign contributions will count towards entitlement for UK benefits on return to the UK. This is not necessarily beneficial, because the foreign contributions then count only for benefits at – usually lower – UK levels.

EC countries

7.57 European Community social security regulations apply to periods spent by UK citizens in other EC member states. The regulations apply only to employees, self-employed persons, and recipients of UK benefits who were formerly employed or self-employed, together with their dependants and survivors. Non-employed people are generally excluded from the scope of the regulations, unless they were formerly employed or self-employed and currently pay Class 3 (voluntary) contributions.

7.58 For employees of a UK employer, UK national insurance contributions continue to be payable where the overseas assignment is for less than 12 months, unless the employee is merely replacing another who has completed a foreign tour of duty. Contributions are not payable to the other EC country's social security scheme, provided a certificate (Form E101) is obtained from the DSS by the UK employer. Once the 12-month period has expired, an extension of up to 12 months can be granted provided the other country's insurance authorities agree. Any extension has to be applied for (on form E102) before the initial 12 months elapse.

7.59 In certain circumstances, an employee may remain within the UK scheme, regardless of the length of the employment in another EC member state. These arrangements, which have to be agreed by the employee and the social security authorities concerned, apply where:

(a) the employee has special knowledge or skills in that job ie his knowledge or skills are not available locally and they are essential to carrying out the job; or
(b) the employer has specific objectives in the country concerned for which the employee's services are required, and the employee is familiar with those objectives.

A certificate E101 must be obtained by the UK employer in these circumstances. Employees satisfying neither (a) nor (b) may still remain within the UK scheme if it is in their interests to do so and the relevant social security authorities agree. In this case, the arrangement will normally be granted only for a fixed period.

7.60 If assigned to work for an employer in another EC country, the employee's liability to pay UK contributions will cease and social security contributions have to be paid under the foreign scheme. If the employment in the UK continues at the same time as the other employment abroad, liability for UK contributions continues if the employee remains ordinarily resident in the UK, or if the employer is based in the UK. Similar rules apply for continuing employment in any of the EC countries other than the UK.

7.61 If the employment is carried out in two or more EC member states, contributions are payable in the member state where the employee resides, in the sense of habitually residing, if his employment has in the past been carried on in that state. Otherwise, liability will generally arise where the employer's place of business or registered office is situated. In the case of multiple employments with different EC employers, liability arises in the member state where the employee resides.

7.62 Where contributions remain payable under the UK scheme, the employee and his dependants may normally claim UK benefits even though they are living in another EC country. It will normally not be possible to claim benefits under the social security scheme of that country unless the individual is insured under that scheme. However, if he is, then past UK contributions will count towards benefits entitlement.

7.63 On return to the UK, contributions paid in another EC country will be taken into account if benefits are claimed in the UK. However, the higher value of contributions paid abroad is reflected in a higher level of benefit only in the case of retirement and widow's pensions. The rules governing individual benefits are complex and further details may be found in booklet SA29, issued by the DSS Overseas Branch.

Visas, residence and work permits

7.64 UK nationals do not require work permits to take up employment in EC countries and may enter these countries on presentation of their passport. A residence permit is required for a stay of more than six months. It will often be necessary to obtain a visa and/or a work permit before entering a non-EC country to work. These documents can normally be obtained at the UK consulate or embassy of the other country.

8 Foreign expatriates in the UK

8.1 It is commonplace nowadays for individuals to be assigned by their employer to work abroad, and the UK is the temporary home of many such expatriates. A considerable number of other expatriates take up residence in the UK to manage and develop their business interests and investments, or choose to live in the UK for personal reasons. The complete absence of exchange controls in the UK is undoubtedly one of the major financial attractions in being based in the UK. Nevertheless, the UK does retain strict immigration controls, so that visas and work permits are necessary for many non-EC nationals. The procedures for obtaining immigration documents are briefly outlined below (see **8.52**), and some useful addresses are given in Appendix 3.

8.2 Taxation is an important consideration for anyone coming to the UK, not merely in the sense that certain tax liabilities may arise but also because there is often scope for mitigating those liabilities by judicious tax planning. The UK possesses a complex and sophisticated tax system, and even those coming from developed countries such as the US will find some fundamental differences from their own tax concepts. It is perhaps a novel concept to foreigners that, in the UK, tax consequences flow to a very large extent from the legal form of transactions, even after the limitations imposed by the *Ramsay* and *Dawson* cases. To ensure that the chosen tax strategy is effective, it is therefore vital to plan in advance so as to have the desired legal arrangements in place at the outset. Advance planning is also necessary from the international point of view, because coming to the UK usually has an effect upon the individual's tax liability in the home country. Any tax planning to take advantage of the move must therefore have regard to those tax considerations as well as to the UK tax aspects. Double taxation relief also needs to be considered. It is essential to co-ordinate any tax advice obtained, and this aim is best facilitated by seeking advice well in advance of making the move.

8.3 In this chapter, the UK tax rules are explained as they affect foreign expatriates generally. The position of expatriate employees is covered in greater detail in chapter 9. For the purposes of these two chapters, it is assumed that the foreign expatriate does not have a UK domicile. For UK domiciled individuals coming from abroad, the tax treatment of overseas income will be as described in chapter 4. It should never be forgotten that taking up residence in the UK is one of the two criteria for acquiring UK domicile of choice. Non-UK domiciled individuals should therefore take care not to demonstrate any intention of remaining indefinitely in the UK if they wish to preserve their fiscally beneficial foreign domicile.

Residence status

8.4 The UK rules on residence are relatively complex, as discussed in chapter 2. For convenience, they are summarised here again. In general, residence is determined on a year-by-year basis. Individuals will be regarded as being resident in the UK for tax purposes for the entire tax year if:

(a) they are physically present in the UK for 183 days or more in total in that tax year: TA 1988 s 336 (IR20 para 8), or

(b) they visit the UK for four consecutive years and their visits average three months or more per annum (IR20 para 21). In these circumstances they will be regarded as resident in the UK in the fifth year or, if such visits were planned from the outset, from the beginning of the first year, or

(c) they have accommodation available for their use in the UK and are present at any time during the tax year for no matter how short a duration (IR20 para 21) (see **2.7**).

8.5 Individuals are not regarded as a resident in the UK in the tax year (6 April to the following 5 April), unless they are physically present at some time during the year (see **2.3**). Residence status is determined separately for husband and wife, although where the couple live together their UK tax residence status will normally be the same. An individual's status under UK immigration laws is generally immaterial to the tax position. Information received by the immigration authorities is not routinely passed on to the Revenue, although taxpayers are sometimes asked to authorise the release of such information. The absence of any automatic information transfer does not of course relieve individuals of the obligation to notify the Revenue if they have any UK tax liabilities resulting from becoming UK resident.

New residents

8.6 As explained in **2.17**, individuals coming to live in the UK are treated as resident from the date of arrival, in certain circumstances: Extra-statutory concession A11. The Revenue practice may be summarised as follows:

(a) new permanent residents: resident and ordinarily resident from date of arrival (IR20 para 19);

(b) individuals intending to reside for at least three years: resident and ordinarily resident from date of arrival (IR20 para 26);

(c) employees visiting for an assignment of at least two but less than three years: resident but not ordinarily resident from date of arrival (IR20 para 25);

(d) visitors for study or education for four years or less: resident but not ordinarily resident from date of arrival (subject to intentions and availability of living accommodation in the UK) (IR20 para 23);

(e) visitors for study or education for more than four years: resident and ordinarily resident from date of arrival (IR20 para 23).

If ordinary residence status is not acquired on arrival, it will be acquired later once the visit to the UK exceeds three years (IR20 para 26) or four years in the case of students: IR20 para 23. A change of intention as to residence may also result in acquisition of ordinary residence.

Domicile

8.7 Domicile of origin is acquired at birth and is normally that of the father (see **3.4**). It is retained by the individual until some positive step is taken to discard it and acquire a new domicile, termed a domicile of choice. It is not easy to acquire a domicile of choice as the domicile of origin has great tenacity (see **3.6**). In effect an individual must be able to demonstrate, to the courts if necessary, that he has adopted a new country as his permanent home. To do this he would have to show that he had broken links with the domicile of origin and established new, firm links with the domicile of choice. Mere transfer of residence is not sufficient to establish a new domicile.

8.8 For individuals whose origin is outside the UK, it is therefore difficult for the tax authorities to show that the domicile of origin has been superseded by a domicile of choice in the UK. Marriage with a UK domiciliary does not necessarily indicate the acquisition of a UK domicile of choice: *IRC v Bullock* [1976] 3 All ER 353, [1976] STC 409. Nevertheless, it is vital for non-domiciled individuals temporarily in the UK to retain as many links as possible – personal, business, social and financial – with their 'home' country. However, for IHT purposes, lengthy residence in the UK may still result in acquisition of a deemed domicile in the UK (see **3.16**).

British emigrés returning to the UK

8.9 If a domicile of choice is abandoned, the domicile of origin automatically revives. This is of special importance to individuals of British origin who have emigrated to another country but are then posted back to the UK to work here. Unless they can convince the Revenue that they have returned only for a temporary reason, they run the risk of being classed as UK domiciled (see **3.12**).

Scope of tax liabilities

8.10 An individual who is resident but not domiciled in the UK is subject to UK taxation as follows:

(a) Income tax:
    (i) UK income: full amount arising
    (ii) Foreign income: amount remitted to the UK.

(b) CGT;
   (i) UK assets: full amount of gains (or losses) realised.
   (ii) Foreign assets: amount of gains remitted to the UK, no relief for losses.
(c) IHT:
   (i) UK assets: subject to IHT.
   (ii) Foreign assets: not subject to IHT.

The position may be modified by the provisions of double taxation agreements.

Year of arrival in the UK

8.11 Change of residence status has no effect upon the basis of assessment of income from a continuing source. On becoming resident, a foreign expatriate will therefore continue to be taxable on UK source income (but see **8.31** below regarding UK bank interest). For example, profits from a UK business in which the individual is a partner will continue to be assessed on the preceding year basis. Sources of foreign income, which will not previously have been subject to UK income tax in the hands of the individual, will become taxable. However, this does not necessarily mean that the commencement basis of assessment applies: *Fry v Burma Corpn Ltd* [1930] AC 321, 15 TC 113, HL. Thus, for (say) rental income from property outside the UK, the assessment for the first year of residence will be based on the income remitted to the UK in the preceding year, assuming that the individual is not UK domiciled. Where there have been no previous remittances, the commencement provisions (see **4.6**) will apply at the time remittances are first made.

8.12 In practice, the strict basis is modified where the individual is a new permanent resident who is treated as resident and ordinarily resident in the UK. If the source of income ceases after the date of arrival but in the same tax year, the assessment is limited to the amount of income arising in the period between arrival and cessation of the income source: IR20 para 69(b).

EXAMPLE

8.13 MN, who is domiciled in France, arrives in the UK on 30 June 1991 for a stay of four years. He is treated as resident and ordinarily resident in the UK from the date of arrival. MN has owned for many years a property in France which is let but this is sold on 30 November 1991. The rental income is as follows:

Year ending 5 April 1991	£ 9,500
Period to 30 November 1991	£ 5,500

Remittances of rental income to the UK are as follows:

Year ending 5 April 1991	£ 2,500
Year ending 5 April 1992	£10,000

Assessment:	Normal basis	Limited to	
1991/92	(CY) £10,000	$\dfrac{5}{8} \times 5,500$	£ 3,437

8.14 If the source ceases in the tax year following arrival, the assessments are limited as follows:

(a) year of arrival: amount of income arising in the basis period for the year, reduced rateably to the period from date of arrival to following 5 April;

(b) Following year: the sum of (i) amount calculated as in (a) for the year of arrival (year 1) plus (ii) income arising in year 2 from 6 April to date source ceases, less the amount actually assessed for year 1.

EXAMPLE

8.15 PQ is domiciled in New Zealand and receives dividends from his shareholding in an Australian company. The shares have been held for several years and dividends have been remitted to a UK bank account since 1980. On 1 August 1991 he comes to the UK to work for five years with a UK company. He sells the shares on 1 June 1992. Dividends paid are as follows:

			Tax year	Amount arising
1 May 1990	£ 5,000	}	1990/91	£8,200
3 November 1990	3,200			
15 May 1991	6,800	}	1991/92	£9,500
20 October 1991	2,700			
4 May 1992	2,000		1992/93	£2,000

Amounts remitted to the UK are:

Year ended 5 April 1991	£ 5,000
Year ended 5 April 1992	2,000
Year ended 5 April 1993	10,000

Assessments:	Normal basis	Limited to
1991/92	(PY) £ 5,000	$\dfrac{8}{12} \times 8,200$ £5,467 (inapplicable)
1992/93	(CY) £10,000	£5,467 + £2,000 − £5,000 = £2,467

8.16 If the source of income ceased before the individual took up permanent residence in the UK, none of the income is taxable in the UK, even if remitted after arrival: IR20 para 69(a). However, there could be liability if the expatriate did not qualify as a new permanent resident and was instead resident from the beginning of the tax year of arrival. In that case, any remittances for that year would be fully taxable if the source of income ceased in that year. To avoid liability, the individual would have to ensure that the source ceased before 6 April in the year of arrival in the UK, in which case there would be no source of income for the year.

8.17 For CGT, there is also a Revenue practice as regards new permanent residents. Provided that the individual has not been resident or ordinarily resident for at least 36 months prior to taking up UK residence, any gains on disposals made before the date of arrival are not subject to CGT: Extra-statutory concession D2, IR20 para 63. For non-UK domiciled expatriates, the result is that capital gains realised before becoming UK resident may be freely remitted to the UK without tax liability, even if the gain was realised in the same tax year as the individual became UK resident.

Tax planning

8.18 To achieve maximum tax benefits from their non-UK domiciled status, foreign expatriates coming to the UK should arrange that, wherever practicable, their non-UK sources of income cease before they become UK resident. Where new permanent resident status is not certain, the income source should cease prior to 6 April in the year of arrival. Clearly, in the case of foreign bank accounts, this can be achieved simply by closing the account and transferring the funds to another bank or branch. The whole of the funds on the new account would then be freely remittable to the UK without UK tax liability. For other income sources, such as property rented, it will often be impractical to effect a disposal and UK tax liability should then be restricted as explained below. For marketable shares and securities, a bed and breakfast transaction should be sufficient to ensure that the previous source of income ceases and a new one commences.

8.19 Where it is not possible to wipe the slate clean by terminating existing sources of foreign income, steps should be taken to isolate those funds which are taxable if remitted to the UK. In a simple case, this would involve the opening of a separate bank account outside the UK to which foreign income is credited after the individual becomes UK resident. Other funds held out-side the UK could then be positively identified as capital, and could be used to make tax free remittances to the UK. For example, interest arising on a foreign bank deposit account should be credited not to that account but to a separate account outside the UK.

8.20 It should be noted that, although there is special treatment for income sources which cease in the year of arrival or the following year (see **8.12**-**8.14**), the basis of assessment is otherwise unchanged. If the source does not cease and remittances were first made to the UK several years earlier, then the assessment for the year of arrival may be made on the amount (if any) remitted in the preceding year, when the individual was not UK resident. Where remittances have only recently started to be made to the UK or where remittances commence on becoming UK resident, the commencement rules apply (see **4.15**). There is no scaling down of the assessment where the individual takes up UK residence part way through the tax year.

8.21   There are 3 main possibilities:

(a) Income first remitted to the UK more than 2 years prior to current tax year. In this case, the preceding year basis applies and the assessment is based on remittances (if any) in the tax year prior to the year of becoming resident.
(b) Income first remitted to the UK in the last but one year before the current year. Here, the basis of assessment for the current year is the amount (if any) remitted to the UK in the immediately preceding year or, if less, the amount remitted in the current year.
(c) Income first remitted to the UK in the immediately preceding year or in the current year. In either case, the assessment for the year in which the individual becomes UK resident is based on the amount of income remitted in that year.

EXAMPLES

8.22   PJ is not domiciled in the UK and has resided overseas for many years. On 30 June 1991 he becomes resident in the UK. He receives rental income from a property which he owns in Spain and this has for a number of years been paid into his bank account in London. Amounts remitted have been as follows:

1987/88	£ 8,000
1988/89	£ 9,500
1989/90	£12,000
1990/91	£15,000
1991/92	£ 5,000

For 1991/92, PJ is assessable under Schedule D Case V on £15,000.

8.23   PK is domiciled in Brazil and becomes resident in the UK on 1 November 1991. He owns shares in a US corporation and in June 1991 remitted £30,000 to the UK out of accumulated dividends as a deposit on a flat in London. No further income is remitted in the year.

For 1991/92, PK is assessable on £30,000 notwithstanding that it is received in the UK in the part of the tax year prior to PK becoming UK resident.

8.24   To the extent that the individual can plan ahead in connection with becoming resident in the UK, remittances to the UK are best avoided in the tax year prior to that in which the individual takes up residence. Alternatively, the preceding year basis can be displaced if the source ceases in the year of arrival. In that case, either the income will be completely free of UK tax (see **8.16**) or the assessment limited as explained in **8.12**.

8.25   A further sophistication is to credit income from different foreign sources to separate accounts outside the UK. The main reason for doing so is that, where income has suffered different rates of foreign tax, the income with the highest foreign tax credit may be remitted in priority to other income. However, it may be difficult to live with such a level of complexity, and the risk of banking error is corresponding higher.

Status rulings

8.26 On arrival in the UK, expatriates should file form P86 (a questionnaire on residence) and a domicile questionnaire in order to obtain a Revenue ruling on their status. It is worth noting that such rulings can often take several weeks to obtain and time should be allowed for this when setting up any tax-related arrangements. It is not uncommon for the Revenue to decline to give a ruling on domicile where they consider that nothing turns upon domicile in computing UK tax liabilities, eg where there are no existing sources of overseas income.

Particular types of foreign income

(see also **4.18–4.24**)

a Income received through UK paying agents

8.27 As mentioned in **6.40**, foreign dividends and other income paid through UK paying or collecting agents may be excluded from the withholding arrangements if the beneficial owner of the income is non-UK resident. If the non-resident becomes UK resident, the withholding requirement is imposed from the date of becoming resident, on payments made after that date: IR20 para 67. Such income is taxable on a current year basis on the gross amount, with a credit for the tax withheld.

8.28 Similarly, payments by UK trustees of income derived from sources outside the UK will become subject to withholding tax once the beneficiary is UK resident. For income arising under foreign trusts, the remittance basis will apply if the beneficiary if non-UK domiciled, provided that the income is not received in the UK through a paying or collecting agent.

b Foreign business income

8.29 Non-UK domiciled individuals are taxed on the remittance basis in respect of the profits of a business or profession carried on outside the UK. As noted in **4.21**, it is likely to be difficult for a UK resident to show that his sole proprietorship is controlled wholly overseas. The case is different with a foreign partnership, where it is quite feasible for non-resident partners to control the business abroad. The UK resident partner's share of profits would then be taxed only if remitted to the UK. One result of a partner taking up residence in the UK might be to create a liability to UK tax if his business activities in the UK on behalf of the partnership amount to earning part of the firm's profits in the UK: TA 1988 s 112(2).

c Foreign pensions

8.30 Foreign pensions received by non-domiciled individuals are taxable on the remittance basis: TA 1988 s 65(4), (5). Lump sum payments from foreign pension funds on completion of overseas duties are not taxable if they relate purely to service outside the UK: IR20 para 66.

UK interest

8.31 The basis of assessment of UK source income is in general unchanged where an individual becomes UK resident (see **8.11**). However, if the individual also becomes ordinarily resident, there is an effect upon the taxation of UK interest income. First, UK bank interest will no longer be receivable gross but must be paid net of basic rate tax (see **6.33**). The individual will be obliged to notify the bank of his change in status. The concession regarding non-assessment of bank interest does not apply for the year of arrival in the UK (see **6.32**). The imposition of withholding at source on the interest is treated as a cessation of the source: TA 1988 s 67(2). The assessment for the year of arrival is therefore based upon the amount of interest arising from 6 April to the date of arrival: TA 1988 s 67(1)(a). In principle, the assessment for the immediately preceding tax year may be increased (see **4.8**), although not if the concession applied to that year. Interest arising on exempt UK government stock (see **1.15**) also becomes subject to withholding from the date of arrival in the UK, although the amount arising before that date is not in practice assessed: IR25 para 62.

UK rental income

8.32 UK rental income which is subject to tax withholding if paid to a non-resident: TA 1988 s 43 (see **6.30**) may become payable gross if the individual becomes UK resident. There is an element of doubt, since the individual's 'usual place of abode' must not be outside the UK and this is not necessarily the same as saying that he is UK resident. The expression 'usual place of abode' is defined elsewhere in the legislation as the country outside the UK in which a person normally lives: TA 1988 s 195(9). Although this definition does not apply for the purposes of s 43, it may be indicative of how the courts would construe the expression. The Revenue appear to regard a usual place of abode as a permanent home, and therefore new permanent residents should be able to avoid the withholding.

Personal allowances

8.33 The fact that an individual is not domiciled in the UK has no effect upon entitlement to personal allowances. For the year of arrival in the UK, a new permanent resident is entitled to full personal allowances: IR20 para 70. The timing of the arrival therefore has a potential benefit in that a full year's allowances can be set-off against only a part year's income.

Deductions and allowances

8.34 Subject to an important exception for expatriate employees (see **9.40**), most payments made by an expatriate qualify for UK tax relief only if they satisfy the normal rules, for example:

(a) interest payments on UK loans to acquire a private residence in the UK (at basic rate only after 1990/91);
(b) maintenance payments to children or a former spouse under a UK court order made before 15 March 1988 (subject to limitations);
(c) premiums paid to UK life offices in respect of pre-14 March 1984 policies;
(d) contributions to approved UK pension funds.

Thus no tax relief is normally given for mortgage interest in respect of a residence outside the UK (but see **9.40**).

Foreign taxation

8.35 The foreign tax implications of becoming UK resident depend upon the detailed tax rules of the country concerned. The fact of being UK resident is not inconsistent with retention of tax residence in another country. A particular example is that of a US citizen, who remains subject to US income tax notwithstanding residence elsewhere. Even if he ceases to be a resident of his country of origin, the expatriate in the UK may well remain taxable on continuing sources of income in that country.

8.36 Where there is double taxation, relief is given as described in **4.35**. A double taxation agreement may give additional relief by way of exemption from tax in the source country, or limitation of the tax rate. For this purpose, it may be necessary to determine residence if the individual is treated both in the UK and in the other country as resident under national tax principles. Where an individual is a resident of two countries, he is entitled to claim relief from third country taxes under any of the tax treaties negotiated by either of his countries of residence. There is no obstacle in principle to his claiming under the treaty giving greater benefits and the Revenue are understood to accept this view.

8.37 In principle, a UK resident can, under a UK tax treaty, obtain relief or exemption from tax in his country of origin. However, such benefits are not available to US citizens resident in the UK, who are taxed in the US as if the US/UK double taxation treaty were not in force. This 'saving' clause is common to all tax treaties negotiated by the US.

8.38 A further restriction on tax treaty relief is that the benefits of the treaty are generally withheld to the extent that the income or gains concerned are taxable in the UK on the remittance basis, but are not in fact remitted. Nevertheless, there can still be benefit in having income taxed in the source country rather than in the UK, since the marginal rate of tax may be less than the corresponding UK rate. Effectively, the total income is split between the UK and the other country, thus tending to reduce the overall rate of tax in each.

Setting up business in the UK

8.39 As mentioned in **8.54**, an individual who comes to the UK to set up his own business will require appropriate entry documents which will give him the authority to set up a business in the UK. An expatriate wishing to establish a UK trade can do this either as a self-employed individual, through a partnership or a company. There are some differences in the tax treatment according to the type of vehicle which is used. The legal formalities of setting up a business, whether corporate or unincorporated, are outside the scope of this work but – broadly speaking – they are relatively straightforward. There are no general restrictions on foreign ownership of UK businesses.

8.40 For the foreign expatriate setting up business in the UK, the main tax implication is that the profits of an unincorporated business will be taxable at his personal income tax rates. Similarly, dividends and director's remuneration from a UK company will be taxable personally to the proprietor. However, individuals who are not domiciled in the UK can achieve an effective reduction of tax on UK business profits by arranging for the business to be carried on either by a UK company owned from abroad eg by a foreign trust or by a non-UK resident company. In this way, profits distributed outside the UK will have borne only UK corporation tax (at rates lower than the top personal income tax rate) and will not be further taxed unless remitted back to the individual in the form of income. This type of arrangement is feasible where the proprietor does not require all the after tax profits to meet UK living expenses, or can remit capital from abroad for this purpose.

EXAMPLE

8.41 JK is resident in but domiciled outside the UK. He sets up a retail business in the UK through a company FGH Ltd. FGH Ltd realises profits of £500,000 for the year ending 31 December 1991, after director's remuneration of £50,000 to JK. The whole of the profit is distributed to the shareholder XYZ SA, resident outside the UK and controlled abroad by non-UK resident members of JK's family.

(a) Profits before tax £500,000
Corporation tax:* 3/12 × 500,000 @ 34% £ 42,500
                  9/12 × 500,000 @ 33% £123,750

166,250

£333,750

*Assuming small companies relief not available

Distribution to XYZ SA	£333,750

ACT payable: 25/75 × 333,750 =	£111,250
fully offset against corporation tax	

(b) If JK had operated as an unincorporated business:

Taxable profits (£500,000 + £50,000)	£550,000

Assuming JK is entitled to a personal allowance of £5,015, his personal tax liability is as follows:

(a) Company:	£ 14,439
(b) Unincorporated business:	£214,439

Total tax for company operations (assuming no tax in XYZ SA on dividends from FGH Ltd) (£166,250 + £14,439)	£180,689

Total tax for unincorporated business	£214,439

Potential tax saving (ignoring national insurance)	£ 33,750

8.42 A similar result would be obtained by trading in the UK using a non-UK resident company, which would however not be subject to ACT on dividends paid. A non-resident company is not entitled to the lower rate of corporation tax on profits up to £1,250,000: TA 1988 s 13, although companies resident in countries with which the UK has concluded a double taxation agreement may be able to claim the lower rate under the non-discrimination provisions of the treaty.

Use of offshore companies and trusts

8.43 An expatriate may decide to invest in the UK through an offshore investment company. One benefit for a non-domiciled individual holding his UK assets through an overseas investment company is that the UK assets owned by the company will not form part of his estate for IHT purposes. This is because the shares in the offshore company are not UK situs property (see **1.11**). The use of legal entities which are resident outside the UK should also minimise exposure to CGT, because there will be no liability except in very limited circumstances (see **1.5**). However, a non-UK resident company will not necessarily escape UK income tax on income arising from UK investments.

8.44 The anti-avoidance rules explained in **4.45** are only of limited application to individuals not domiciled in the UK. There will be no tax charge unless the income arising to the offshore entity would have been taxable had it arisen directly to the individual: TA 1988 s 743(3). Consequently, foreign source income not remitted to the UK is not apportioned to the individual concerned, even if it is used to make benefits available to him in the UK. Moreover, a foreign expatriate coming to the UK having previously set up an offshore fund or settlement may often be able to rely on the defence that the arrangements were made for purposes other than avoidance of UK tax: TA 1988 s 741.

8.45 For CGT, the usual rules regarding apportionment of capital gains realised by non-resident closely held companies (see **4.48**) and non-resident trusts (see **4.50**) are inapplicable to non-UK domiciled individuals: CGTA 1979 s 15(2), FA 1981 s 80(6). The attribution of the gains of a non-resident trust to the settlor does not apply unless the settlor is UK resident and domiciled at the same time during the tax year concerned: FA 1991 Sch 16 para 1(1)(*c*).

Capital tax protection

8.46 Arrangements set up to protect assets against UK capital taxes could in principle involve either a foreign company or a non-UK resident trust. In both cases, the property so held can be excluded from IHT. However, a settlement is excluded only if:

(a) the settled property is situated outside the UK and
(b) the settlor was not UK domiciled immediately before the settlement was made: IHTA 1984 s 48(3).

Where the UK property is to be settled, it should therefore be owned by a foreign company, the shares in which are held by the non-resident trustees. In the latter case, capital gains realised by the company can be attributed to the trustees, although no gains can be further apportioned to non-UK domiciled beneficiaries.

8.47 On balance, a foreign settlement is likely to be a more effective long-term arrangement for capital tax protection. It may be difficult to ensure that a foreign company remains non-resident if it is owned and managed by a UK resident, and this could create a CGT exposure. The IHT position is also doubtful, because there are indications that shares in a UK-resident company could be treated as UK situs property, notwithstanding its incorporation outside the UK: *Bradbury v English Sewing Cotton Co Ltd* [1923] AC 744, 8 TC 481, HL. The risks can be obviated where control rests with the non-resident trustees. Moreover, the property comprised in the settlement never becomes subject to IHT even if the settlor subsequently becomes UK domiciled, or is deemed to be so under the special IHT rules (see **3.16**). This assumes that the settlement is an effective transfer for IHT. The position is doubtful if the settlor retains an interest in the settled property, eg as a discretionary beneficiary. This might be treated as a reservation of benefit, so that the settled property would form part of the estate on death if the settlor was then UK domiciled: FA 1986 s 102.

8.48 The use of a foreign company to own UK real estate may present additional problems. The tax charge on living accommodation provided to employees and directors (see **9.14**) may apply where, as is not uncommon, the UK property is a house or apartment occupied by the expatriate. Even though the individual may not formally be a director or employee of the foreign company concerned, he might still be de facto a director, as a person in accordance with whose instructions the directors are accustomed to act: TA 1988 s 168(5). Whilst it is arguable that a person who is merely a shadow director is not caught by the benefits rules as no employment is involved, there is no simple method of avoiding such a line of attack by the Revenue, although there is merit in divesting the individual of control by having the company owned by independent non-resident trustees who appoint the directors.

8.49 A further possibility inherent in non-resident settlements created by non-UK domiciliaries is the avoidance of CGT on overseas assets. If the assets are gifted in settlement to non-resident trustees, even with the settlor as one of the beneficiaries, no CGT liability arises. Any gains are taxable on the remittance basis and, because there are no proceeds, no remittances are possible. If the trustees subsequently dispose of the assets, and distribute the proceeds to the settlor or other non-UK domiciled beneficiaries under the trust, no CGT liability arises: FA 1981 s 80(6). In other words, the assets can – in theory – be sold and the proceeds remitted to the original owner, free of UK tax. Nevertheless, if the settlement is made purely to avoid CGT on an impending third party sale, there is a risk that the ruling in *Furniss v Dawson* would be applied to ignore the fiscal consequences of the inter-mediate transfers: see *Young v Phillips* [1984] STC 520. There are rules which attribute gains of overseas trusts formed on or after 19 March 1991 to the settlor: FA 1991 s 89, Sch 16, but they apply only where the settlor is both UK domiciled and either resident or ordinarily resident in the tax year concerned.

Social security and benefits

8.50 Foreign expatriates coming to the UK are in general subject to national insurance contribution liability from the date of arrival. The posi-tion of employed individuals is described more fully in chapter 9. Self-employed individuals are required to pay a weekly flat rate contribution (Class 2) and an earnings related element (Class 4), 50% of the latter being tax deductible. Other expatriates may pay a voluntary non-employed flat rate contribution (Class 3) but this secures only limited benefits and is arguably not worth paying.

8.51 Foreign nationals are not in general entitled to claim UK social security benefits unless they have made appropriate contributions under UK rules. However, there are a number of reciprocal social security agreements (see **7.53**) under which expatriates who are nationals of one of the countries concerned may claim UK benefits, including free medical treatment under the National Health Service.

Visas

8.52 The UK imposes restrictions on immigration, and foreign nationals may require entry visas and residence permits. The position regarding work permits is explained in Chapter 9.

8.53 EC nationals do not require visas or work permits to visit or take up employment in the UK and may enter the country on presentation of their passport. If they wish to stay for more than 6 months they should furnish the Home Office with a certificate from their employer and they will be granted a resident permit valid for five years (or the duration of the assignment if less than 12 months) which may be renewed.

8.54 When an employer does not have a UK base, the individual should obtain a letter of consent from a British Embassy or Consulate overseas to obtain entry to the UK as a sole representative. A letter of consent entitles an individual to stay in the UK for an initial 12-month period which may be renewed. If these renewals exceed a 4-year period the Home Office may grant permanent residence. The individual then acquires the right of abode in the UK and is no longer required to demonstrate a link with the foreign employer.

8.55 A person seeking to set up in business (including self-employment in the UK) must obtain an entry clearance. He must show that:

(a) he has at least £150,000 under his control in the UK which will be invested in the business;
(b) the investment made will, if he is not the sole owner, be proportionate to his interest in the business;
(c) he is in a position to bear the appropriate proportion of liabilities;
(d) he will be actively involved in running the business, on a full-time basis;
(e) there is a need for his services and for the proposed investment;
(f) new full-time employment will be provided in the UK, in the case of a new business.

8.56 Another category of residence permit may be granted for individuals of independent means. It is necessary for the individual to show that he has independent financial status, and possession of disposable assets exceeding £150,000 in value, or income of at least £15,000 a year, is accepted as adequate evidence of this. It is also necessary to demonstrate a family or other personal link with the UK before a permit will be granted under this category.

9 Expatriate employees in the UK

9.1 The territorial basis of taxation of employment income is as set out in **5.2**. For individuals not domiciled in the UK, the main additional aspect is the remittance basis for certain foreign service contracts (see **9.7**). The remittance basis is relevant only to foreign emoluments, which are earnings arising under a service contract where the employer is resident outside the UK (and not resident in the UK), and the employee is not UK domiciled: TA 1988 s 192(1). The apparently double exclusion of UK resident employers is somewhat curious, since it is rare that a company can be resident both in the UK and elsewhere on the basis of the UK criterion of central management and control: see *Swedish Central Rly Co Ltd v Thompson* [1925] AC 495, 9 TC 342, HL. A dually resident company, such as a US corporation resident (ie managed and controlled) in the UK is normally resident only in the UK for UK tax purposes. A company incorporated in the UK is ipso facto UK resident, subject to exceptions for companies incorporated and carrying on business before 15 March 1988: TA 1988 s 66(1), Sch 7. Foreign emoluments cannot arise from employment with a person resident in the Republic of Ireland: TA 1988 s 192(1).

9.2 The foreign emoluments deduction – which had previously been available generally to all expatriate employees – ceased to be available to expatriates from 1990/91 onwards.

Expatriates not ordinarily resident in the UK

9.3 For individuals who are not ordinarily resident in the UK (see **2.11**), UK income tax is charged under two headings (see **5.2**). For UK duties, the charge is under Schedule E Case II in respect of remuneration attributable to those duties, on the amount of the emoluments received in the tax year in respect of the duties, whether received in the UK or elsewhere: TA 1988 s 202A (see **5.7–5.9**). Remuneration for non-UK duties is taxed only on amounts remitted to the UK, under Schedule E Case III.

9.4 In these circumstances, it is not necessary for there to be separate contracts for UK and overseas duties. Remuneration arising under a single contract is apportioned rateably to the numbers of working days spent in the UK and abroad respectively: Statement of Practice SP5/84. Where the remuneration is paid wholly outside the UK, the Revenue regard any remittances primarily as relating to UK duties, so that a further tax charge arises only where the remittances exceed the remuneration attributable to those duties. Similarly, where part of the remuneration is paid in the UK, remittances of the earnings paid overseas are taxable only to the extent that the UK payments plus the remittances exceed remuneration for the UK duties: SP5/84 para 5.

9.5 Individuals who are resident but not ordinarily resident will by implication be resident only temporarily in the UK, perhaps for relatively short periods each year. It is possible in such circumstances that the individual would remain resident in another country. A claim for exemption from UK tax may then be competent, under the terms of a double taxation agreement. However, it is necessary to resolve the question of dual residence for treaty purposes under the relevant tie breaker clause in the treaty (see **2.22**). In the event that the individual is deemed to be resident in the other country, he is entitled to claim exemption from UK tax, notwithstanding that he remains resident in the UK for UK domestic tax purposes.

9.6 The exemption would relate to emoluments for non-UK duties, since the UK's taxing rights are generally limited to emoluments for duties performed in the UK. Emoluments for UK duties can be exempt as well, provided that the individual is present in the UK for less than 183 days in the tax year and the employer is not UK resident and the earnings are not borne by a UK branch of the employer (see **5.42**).

Overseas employment contracts

9.7 For employees who are resident and ordinarily resident income tax is chargeable on worldwide remuneration under Schedule E Case I. The basis of taxation of non-UK domiciled employees is different for remuneration arising under a separate contract relating solely to non-UK duties with a non-UK resident employer. In that case, UK tax is charged under Case III on earnings from the contract that are remitted to the UK: TA 1988 s 192(2). This usually makes it desirable to arrange for a separate contract to govern any non-UK duties, so that there is the opportunity to avoid UK income tax on the overseas element if the employee does not need to remit it to the UK.

9.8 It is not entirely straighforward to arrange matters in this way. The UK tax authorities are often reluctant to accept that there can be two separate employment contracts with a single employer, especially if the nature of the duties specified under each is similar. For this reason, it is advisable for UK and non-UK contracts to be with different employers, such as sister companies within the same group. Even if the contracts are accepted as genuine, there are powers for the UK Revenue to adjust the earnings arising under each to prevent artificially high loading to the foreign contract: TA 1988 s 192(5), Sch 12 paras 2(2), (3). It is also sensible to make sure that adequate earnings arise under the UK contract to meet UK expenses.

9.9 Avoidance of UK income tax on overseas income by remitting it to the UK in a tax year after the source has ceased to exist (see **8.16**) is not now possible in the case of employment income under Schedule E Case III. The remittance is taxable whether the earnings are for the year of remittance or for some earlier (or later) year, and regardless of whether the employment is still in existence at the time of the remittance: TA 1988 s 202A(2). However, no tax charge would arise if the individual was not UK resident for the tax year in which the remittance was made, because UK residence is a prerequisite for assessment under Schedule E Case III. Alternatively, exemption from UK tax might be available under a double taxation agreement (see **9.5**). Thus, if an overseas employer was prepared to pay the employee in advance for duties to be performed under a foreign contract, these earnings could be remitted to the UK tax-free prior to the employee taking up residence in the UK.

Duties outside the UK

9.10   The treatment of earnings for duties outside the UK depends upon residence status and, in some cases, on the contractual arrangements which apply. The following table summarises the position.

Employee's status	*Earnings for non-UK duties*
Not resident	Not taxable
Resident, not ordinarily resident	Taxable on amounts remitted to UK
Resident and ordinarily resident	Taxable on full amount arising*

*See also **9.7**

Overseas earnings deductions

9.11   For non-domiciled persons employed by a UK resident employer the remittance basis is not available. However, provided the individual is both resident and ordinarily resident in the UK, the 100% deduction may be claimed for duties performed wholly or partly outside the UK in the course of a qualifying period of 365 days or more (see **5.28**). Many foreign nationals who would be able to meet the terms of the 100% deduction could probably arrange not to be resident in the UK for tax purposes or, at least, to be resident in another country for the purposes of a double taxation agreement (see **9.5**).

Double taxation relief

9.12   If the country in which the overseas duties are carried out taxes the employee, then this foreign tax will be allowed as a credit against the UK tax liability on the same income, ignoring any special deduction given for UK tax purposes. If earnings are taxed in the UK on the remittance basis, the attributable foreign tax is found by grossing up the remittances at the average rate of foreign tax on that income. In the alternative, relief from foreign tax may be claimed under the terms of a UK tax treaty. However, under most UK double tax treaties, income of UK residents which is taxed on the remittance basis is disqualified from relief or exemption from foreign tax unless remitted to the UK.

Expenses and benefits

9.13 A brief survey of the main rules relating to the taxation of expenses and benefits in kind is given in **5.11–5.12**. These rules are applicable equally to expatriate personnel working in the UK. Expenses paid and benefits made available outside the UK are in principle taxable on the individual if he is a director or is paid at an annual rate of more than £8,500 a year including all taxable benefits. If the employee's foreign earnings are taxable on the remittance basis, benefits made available and expenses paid outside the UK, relating to the overseas duties, will not normally be taxed. However, importation to the UK of property representing non-UK benefits is likely to be treated as a remittance of the foreign earnings, in view of the wide definition of remittances for Schedule E (see **1.18**).

Housing costs

9.14 The provision of a residence for an employee (whether higher paid or not) or director, is taxable on the greater of the annual rental value as defined, or the actual rent payable by the employer (see **5.13**). There is an additional taxable benefit on accommodation which cost the employer more than £75,000. The excess of the actual cost over £75,000 is multiplied by the 'official rate' of interest at the beginning of the tax year (see **9.23**) and this notional rent is added to the annual value of the property: TA 1988 s 146. Thus, for a house costing £150,000 with an annual value of £1,000, the benefit would be £11,125 for 1991/92 (the official rate at 6 April 1991 being 13.5%). 'Cost' for this purpose usually means purchase price plus the cost of improvements, but if the property has been owned by the employer for more than six years before the employee moves in, the market value of the property at the latter date is substituted for cost. The substitution of market value does not apply where the employee first occupied the accommodation before 1 April 1983. Although the taxable benefit is reduced by the employee's rental contribution, it is conceivable that even a full market rental would not eliminate the taxable benefit for some houses costing over £75,000 because the benefit is calculated using an interest rate, not a rental yield.

9.15 There are three exemptions from the tax charge (TA 1988 s 145(3):

(a) when it is necessary for the employee to reside in the accommodation for the proper performance of his duties (for example, a hotel manager);
(b) where the accommodation is provided for the better performance of his duties and it is customary for living accommodation to be provided in similar employment (for example, a house-master at a boarding school);
(c) where there is a security threat and the employee resides in the property as part of security arrangements.

9.16 Should the employer also bear the cost of ancillary expenses (eg heating, lighting, furniture and repairs) the full cost is chargeable to tax unless the director or employee comes within one of the three exemptions, in which case the benefit is limited to 10% of the net amount of the employee's or director's compensation: TA 1988 s 163. If the employer also pays the community charge in respect of the property, there is a tax liability on the employee if the liability relates to his personal community charge (ie the property is his only or main residence). If the standard charge is payable, the Revenue regard this as falling within Extra-statutory concession A5 (see **9.29**), provided that the relevant conditions are satisfied.

9.17 Although there is special relief from tax on the cost of board and lodging for UK employees working overseas: TA 1988 s 193(4) (see **5.25**), no analogous relief is given in respect of board and lodging provided to expatriate employees working in the UK. Relief was proposed in Revenue consultative papers issued in 1984 and 1985, but not proceeded with. In practice, it may be possible to persuade the inspector not to tax the cost of UK living accommodation provided for a temporary stay in the UK, especially if the employee retains a home overseas which continues to be occupied by his family. If the employee moves to the UK, and the cost of accommodation equivalent to that in the home country is more expensive, payments received from the employer to compensate for the additional cost are tax free by concession, to to an overall limit equal to the current Civil Service maximum: Extra-statutory concession A67.

Travel and subsistence expenses

9.18 Travel and associated costs are deductible if incurred on a business journey. Expenses of travel between the employee's home and his usual place of work are not deductible although there may be room for argument if an employee works from home: *Owen v Pook* [1970] AC 244, 45 TC 571, HL. If an employee uses his own car for business travel then he may claim for reasonable expenses relating to the actual business use; the simplest way to deal with this is for the employer to pay a fixed rate per business mile, although a taxable benefit may arise if the employee's business mileage is high (see TA 1988 ss 197A–197F). If the employer provides the car for the employee's use, different provisions apply (see **9.22**).

9.19 Special reliefs apply to travel costs of non-UK domiciled employees performing UK duties: TA 1988 s 195. To qualify, the employee must not have been UK resident in either of the 2 tax years preceding the tax year in which he arrives in the UK to take up the UK duties, and must not have been present in the UK for any purpose in the 2 year period ending with the date of arrival: TA 1988 s 195(3). The latter condition seem unnecessarily harsh, in that it would preclude relief if the individual had merely taken a holiday in the UK in the 2 year period, wholly unconnected with the employment. Where relief does apply, it covers expenses for a period of 5 years beginning with the date of arrival: TA 1988 s 195(2). If there are successive assignments to the UK in the same tax year, the earliest date of arrival is the relevant date for this purpose.

9.20 The relief covers the cost of travel

(a) from the employee's usual place of abode overseas to any place in the UK for the purpose of performing duties there;
(b) from any place in the UK to his usual place of abode after performing the duties: TA 1988 s 195(5).

In practice, the Revenue treat the relief as including subsistence costs incurred in the course of qualifying journeys eg accommodation whilst in transit. The employee's usual place of abode is the place overseas where he normally lives: TA 1988 s 195(9). To qualify for relief, expenses must be paid for directly by the employer or, if paid by the employee, reimbursed to him. An apportionment is made for journeys made partly for purposes other than (a) or (b) above. It is debatable whether this relief in strictness extends to the journey from the airport to the individual's temporary home in the UK, since the wording of the legislation implies that the duties must be performed at the destination location. Also, in contrast to the relief for UK employees travelling abroad (see **5.20**), there is no specific relief for the cost of intermediate return trips home, where paid for by the employer.

9.21 In addition, relief is available for the costs of visits to the UK by the employee's spouse and children, where met by the employer, but only if the employee is in the UK for a continuous period of 60 days or more: TA 1988 s 195(6). The cost of a journey to accompany the employee to the UK is also included. The relief applies only to 2 journeys each way per tax year per person. As in the case of the employee's travel, the employer must meet the cost directly or reimburse the employee, and the cost of dual-purpose journeys is apportioned.

Company cars

9.22 Where the director or higher paid employee has a company car available for his private use, a notional annual benefit is calculated by reference to a statutory fixed scale (which varies from year to year) based on the cylinder capacity and/or the retail value of the car when new. If the annual business mileage is less than 2,500 miles the taxable benefit is 1½ times the scale rate. This increase also applies to a second car provided, whether or not the minimum mileage is achieved. Where annual business mileage is 18,000 or more, the scale rate is reduced by one half. There is an additional tax charge, also on a fixed scale where the employer meets the cost of the invidual's private petrol consumption. A fixed benefit is assessed in respect of a mobile telephone provided by the employer: TA 1988 s 159A.

Employer loans

9.23 If a loan is granted to a director or employee interest free, or at a rate lower than commercial interest rates, then a taxable benefit can arise calculated on the difference between the actual interest paid by the employee and that which he would have paid if the 'official rate' had been applied: TA 1988 s 160. The official rate is fixed by statutory instrument and varies in line with market rates of interest for sterling. There is no special provision for foreign currency loans. Imputed amounts of £300 or less are not taxed but there is no marginal relief where the cash equivalent exceeds £300: TA 1988 s 161(1). The de minimis amount was £200 up to 1990/91. Employee loans are not taxable if any interest paid would normally qualify for tax relief. However, there is a complication in the case of house purchase loans, where tax relief is available only at the basic rate of income tax on interest relating to the first £30,000 of the loan. Special adjustments are required to preserve the higher rate tax charge in this case: TA 1988 Sch 7 Part IV. There are also complex rules dealing with the case where interest would have been partly tax deductible if paid and where the amount of loan changes during the year.

9.24 A loan granted outside the UK by an employer to an expatriate employee is in principle within the scope of the above rules. However, if the employee is taxable only under Schedule E Case III in respect of overseas duties, it might be possible to attribute the benefits wholly to overseas duties and thus escape UK tax on the interest foregone. The benefit of an interest-free or low interest UK loan eg for house purchase will invariably be taxable. If the loan is wholly or partly written off, the amount written off is a taxable benefit in kind. Where the write off occurs after the UK contract has terminated, the benefit remains taxable under Schedule E: TA 1988 s 160. It is doubtful whether the employee's ceasing to be UK resident affects the tax treatment of such a benefit, since it is not taxable under any specified Case of Schedule E.

School fees

9.25 Should an employer meet the school fees of the children of the director or employee, then the amount actually paid by the employer will be taxed as a benefit on the director or employee: TA 1988 s 154. It might be possible for an expatriate to avoid this tax charge if the cost of schooling is necessitated purely by the UK assignment; for example, where the children are boarders at a school abroad, or attend a foreign school whilst in the UK.

Training

9.26 The costs of training are, by concession, free of tax where the training is for the acquisition of skills directly related to the increased effectiveness of the employee in performing the duties of the employment: Extra-statutory concession A63. The Revenue seem to accept that this concession extends to the cost of English language tuition for foreigners coming to work in the UK.

Medical insurance

9.27 For higher paid directors and employees, the cost of medical insurance premiums (eg under BUPA type schemes) borne by the employer is taxable. The costs of medical treatment whilst the employee is working outside the UK, or insurance premiums in connection with such costs, are not taxable: TA 1988 s 155(6).

Home country expenses

9.28 Where an employee maintains a home abroad for his family or dependants, he will be unlikely to obtain any UK tax deduction for the associated expenses. It may be possible to claim relief for mortgage interest payments on the basis that they are 'corresponding' payments, that is, that they would have been allowable had they been paid in the UK in respect of a residence here (see **9.40** below). Other continuing commitments abroad, such as social security contributions, will not be tax deductible in the UK even if they would have been in the home country.

Removal expenses

9.29 Any reimbursement or payment of removal expenses by the employer is in principle taxable on the employee. In practice the Revenue will allow such expenses provided they are borne by the employer, are reasonable in amount and their payment is properly controlled: Extra-statutory concession A5 (see **7.10**). It is also necessary that they have been occasioned because the employee has to change his residence on first joining an organisation or because of a transfer to another job within an organisation. The allowable removal expenses would also include a temporary subsistence allowance until the employee finds permanent accommodation. There are no fixed guidelines and it is a matter for negotiation in particular cases. This practice will apply where an expatriate is moving to a new house in the UK which he is responsible for furnishing. The Revenue do not generally apply the concession unless the former residence is disposed of, although it may apply when the employee moves back to his overseas residence on termination of his UK contract.

Entertainment expenses or allowances

9.30 The cost of entertaining is invariably disallowable for UK tax, even if there are genuine business reasons for the expenses being incurred: TA 1988 s 577. Where an employee provides entertainment in a business context, Revenue practice is to disallow the expense for the employer but not to tax the expense on the employee. The expenses must be actually paid or reimbursed by the employer.

Spouse expenses

9.31 Even for bona fide business trips, expenses of an accompanying spouse are allowable only if it can be shown there is some business necessity for their presence: *Maclean v Trembath* [1956] 2 All ER 113, 36 TC 653. In that case it was held that the expenses attributable to the wife were not allowable. A deduction may be able to be claimed if the spouse is required to act as host/hostess for necessary business entertaining on the particular trip. Alternatively, the spouse might genuinely assist at a professional level in the business, or the employee might be in poor health and should not travel alone (see Extra-statutory concession A5). Spouse expenses can be difficult to support as a tax deduction and it is always wise to ensure that the expenses are properly documented and authorised by the employer.

Tax equalisation

9.32 Many employers undertake to compensate expatriate employees for the cost of foreign taxes. Sometimes the protection extends only to the amount by which the foreign tax exceeds tax in the home country on an equivalent remuneration package (tax equalisation) (see **5.44**). In the UK, payment of any part of the employee's UK tax liability is itself a taxable benefit and thus the equivalent amount of taxable earnings has to be calculated on a grossed up basis. This can be a complex exercise, although there now exist a number of computer programs designed to carry out the necessary calculations.

EXAMPLE

9.33 J is seconded to the UK by his overseas employer. In his country of residence, his net remuneration after tax would have been the equivalent of £50,000. J's employer undertakes that his net UK earnings after tax for 1991/92 will be £50,000.

Net earnings		£50,000
Personal allowance for 1991/92	£ 5,015	
Basic rate earnings after tax for 1991/92		
£23,700 – 25% × £23,700	17,775	
		(22,790)
Higher rate earnings after tax for 1991/92		27,210
Gross up for tax at 40%		18,140
		45,350
National insurance contributions (employee)	1,636	
Gross up for tax at 40%	1,091	
		2,727
Personal allowance		5,015
Basic rate earnings (gross)		23,700
Equivalent gross earnings		£76,792

Stock option and incentive schemes

9.34   Issue of a stock option to employees does not normally give rise to an immediate tax charge, but taxable income arises instead when the option is exercised: TA 1988 s 135. It is immaterial whether the option relates to shares in a UK or in a foreign company. However, individuals coming to the UK may often avoid UK tax on the exercise of options previously acquired. That is because gains from exercising a stock option are treated as taxable earnings only if it is granted to an individual by reason of an employment the earnings from which are within Schedule D Case I: TA 1988 s 140(1). Thus, the tax charge does not apply unless the employee was resident and ordinarily resident at both the time of the grant and of the exercise of the option. Alternatively, the tax charge can be avoided by UK resident employees who are not UK domiciled and are in receipt of foreign emoluments taxable under Schedule E Case III.

9.35   Stock options issued while the employee is UK resident and exercised free of tax after the UK assignment has terminated may still be taxable even if the employee is then non-resident (see **7.26**). Revenue practice appears to be that liability is not pursued where the period of UK residence was relatively brief and the options concerned related to shares in a foreign company. Foreign tax considerations should be taken into account in the latter case, although it may be possible to exercise the options before becoming tax resident in another country.

9.36   If a scheme involves the issue of shares to an employee at less than market value, but without any option being involved, the amount of the undervalue is treated as an additional emolument. The use of restrictions to depress market value may avoid an initial tax charge but any gain arising when the restrictions are lifted or the shares are disposed of (or on the seventh anniversary of the date of acquisition, if earlier) will be taxable as income. The latter provision is, however, applicable only to Case I employments, as for share options: FA 1988 s 77(2) (see **7.30**).

9.37   A further tax drawback in using a share incentive scheme is that, for directors and higher paid employees, the amount of any undervalue on issue of shares is treated as a notional loan subject to the deemed interest provision already outlined: TA 1988 s 162. The loan is treated as written off if the shares are disposed of or, if issued as partly paid, are made fully paid without full payment being made by the employee. The amount written off is then treated as taxable income. The tax charges just described are not dependent on residence status at the time of issue of the shares and can catch share issues made before the employee became UK resident.

9.38   There are special types of tax effective employee participation schemes but they are of limited value to expatriates because of the relatively low annual ceiling on the value of shares that can be allocated, the minimum holding period between grant of the option and its exercise, and the restriction of such schemes to shares in UK companies.

Pension benefits

9.39 Pension contributions made by the expatriate's employer will normally be taxable if the pension scheme operated is not one approved by the Inland Revenue. If the scheme is a foreign one, it may be possible to obtain a tax deduction if the provisions of the scheme correspond broadly to those of a UK approved scheme (see **9.40**): TA 1988 s 192(3), IR25 para 3.17. The payment of contributions by the employee may also be deductible, on a similar basis. Any contributions paid by employees to an approved UK pension fund will be tax deductible from the employees' earnings. Although a foreign employer can set up a UK approved pension scheme, there has to be a UK-resident trustee. Commercially, the creation of such a scheme is unattractive unless there are a significant number of long-term UK-based employees.

Corresponding payments

9.40 Expatriates in receipt of foreign emoluments (see **9.1**) may claim a tax deduction for payments that do not in strictness qualify under UK tax rules but which would do so but for the fact of being paid abroad: TA 1988 s 192(3). In practice, the Revenue interpretation of 'corresponding payments' is rather wider than the statute would suggest, and the following should qualify:

(a) interest paid abroad in respect of the individual's private residence overseas;
(b) alimony payments made under a foreign court order, but only to the limited extent available for UK maintenance payments;
(c) premiums on a life policy with a foreign life office: IR25 para 3.17.

It would appear that, under (c), only pre 14 March 1984 policies would qualify (see **1.32**).

9.41 The main restriction on the deduction of corresponding payments is that they are deemed to be met primarily out of overseas income not charged to UK tax, such as investment income and remuneration taxed on the remittance basis. Capital resources outside the UK are ignored for this purpose.

Termination payments

9.42 Expatriates whose service contracts are terminated whilst they are UK resident may be taxable on any compensation or ex-gratia payment received: TA 1988 s 148. Payments up to £30,000 are free of UK income tax.

9.43 Foreign expatriates may be entitled to additional relief for foreign service, defined as duties for which the remuneration

(a) was not taxable under Schedule E Case I, or
(b) attracted the 100% special deduction (see **5.28**): TA 1988 s 188(3) Sch 11 para 10.

The relief consists of a total exemption where the length of foreign service was

(i) 75% of the total period of service, or
(ii) (if total service exceeds 10 years) the whole of the last 10 years, or
(iii) (if total service exceeds 20 years), 50% of the whole period, including any 10 of the last 20 years of service: TA 1988 s 188(3)(b).

The Revenue in practice aggregate all service with companies in the same group when considering this exemption.

9.44 If full exemption is unavailable, the relief given is a rateable proportion of the termination payment, by reference to the number of years of foreign service out of the total period of service with the employer or group: TA 1988 Sch 11 para 3. The strict legal position is unclear, but in practice the Revenue deduct the foreign service relief before considering the £30,000 exemption.

9.45 The tax treatment of termination payments received after ceasing to be UK resident is unclear. The legislation directs that such payments are to be assessed under Schedule E but does not specify which Case is applicable. For a non resident, Case II is the only possible Case applicable but it relates expressly to emoluments for duties performed in the UK. There is therefore a risk that expatriates whose employment is terminated after a UK assignment may in principle be subject to UK income tax on at least part of the payment. The effect of double taxation agreements is obscure, since termination payments do not necessarily rank as employment income for the purposes of the treaty. Exemption may, however, be due if the treaty contains an article covering 'other income' (see **1.43**). The date of termination of the service contract, not the date of payment, is the effective date for UK tax purposes: TA 1970 s 148(4).

Tax withholding

9.46 An obligation is imposed upon employers to withhold income tax and national insurance contributions from cash remuneration paid to employees, in accordance with the rules of the Pay-As-You-Earn (PAYE) scheme: TA 1988 s 203. Obligations under PAYE extend to non-UK resident employers: *Clark v Oceanic Contractors Inc* [1983] 1 All ER 133, [1983] STC 35. In practice, employers having no business establishment in the UK are not normally required to operate PAYE and employees can account for their own tax under a direct collection (DC) procedure. Under the DC system, an estimated assessment is made on the employee, requiring tax to be paid quarterly. Any difference either way is dealt with at the end of the year, once the individual's actual liability is known. Where an expatriate employee is seconded to a UK company, the Revenue often press for the UK company to operate PAYE. Such requests can sometimes be resisted if the UK company is not responsible for paying the expatriate and it is desirable to keep details of their remuneration confidential from UK personnel. Nevertheless, where the employee is under the general management and control of the UK company, that company is in strictness treated as the employer for PAYE purposes: Income Tax (Employments) Regulations 1973 SI 1973/334, reg 3.

Social security and benefits

9.47 The UK has a contributory social security system, national insurance. Contributions for employed persons are earnings related and are payable on full earnings (where above a very low minimum level) subject to a ceiling which is raised annually in line with the percentage increase in average earnings. Contributions are payable both by the employee and employer, but there is no upper earnings limit for employer's contributions. The rates of contribution and the earnings limits vary from year to year. The employer's contributions are deductible in computing business profits, in the same way as wages and salaries, but the employee's contribution is not tax deductible. Contributions from employed persons are normally collected by withholding from salary payments, along with tax under PAYE (see **9.46**).

9.48 Contributions are also payable by self-employed persons. There is a flat rate contribution and also an earnings related contribution based on taxable profits falling within a prescribed band. The flat rate contribution is payable directly but the earnings related element is included in the notice of tax assessment on business profits. One half of the earnings-related contribution is tax deductible: TA 1988 s 617(5).

Individuals coming to the UK

9.49 For individuals coming to work temporarily in the UK there may be an exemption from payment of contributions for the first 52 weeks of their stay. The exemption applies where:

(a) the employee was not ordinarily resident in the UK immediately before his arrival; and
(b) the employer is not resident in the UK; and
(c) the employer has a place of business outside the UK.

Non-residents who are non-executive directors of UK companies are in principle liable to Class I contributions on their fees, although the DSS do not pursue liability where the only UK activities are to attend no more than 10 board meetings a year, none of which lasts more than 2 days, or no more than 1 board meeting a year which does not last more than 2 weeks.

9.50 'Ordinarily resident' for this purpose is defined somewhat differently than for income tax purposes. Broadly speaking, a foreign national is not ordinarily resident in the UK at a given date if he has not been resident in the UK at any time during the three years preceding that date.

9.51 The exemption extends to both employer's and employee's contributions. Thereafter, the employee's contribution becomes payable, subject to any further exemption as described below, but the employer is not liable unless he is then resident or present in the UK or has a place of business in the UK. 'Presence' in the UK would include a representative office which did not carry on business. It is arguable that the 52 week exemption period recommences if the employee leaves the UK and subsequently returns to the UK, even if the period spent abroad is relatively short, provided that he remains non-ordinarily resident immediately prior to his return.

9.52 On arrival in the UK, foreign nationals must register with the social security authorities (DSS), completing form CF8 and producing evidence of identity (passport and – for non-EC nationals – work permit). The DSS insist that these formalities are completed at the relevant DSS office and they do not accept postal applications. Completion of form CF8 results in the issue of a national insurance number which plays a vital role in the PAYE procedure for deduction of tax and national insurance contributions. As the information given on the form also affects entitlement to the 52 week exemption it is important to consult professional advisers before attending the DSS office.

EC nationals

9.53 EC nationals seconded by their employer to work in the UK remain subject to social security contributions in their own country, if the secondment is for 12 months or less. This exemption applies even if the employer has a place of business in the UK. Form E101 should be obtained from the relevant social security office in the home country before leaving. If the secondment unexpectedly lasts more than 12 months (but not more than 24 months) the exemption period may be extended if the DSS agree. Form E102 must be obtained and submitted to the UK overseas group social security office before the end of the initial 12-month period. These exemptions do not apply to employees replacing others who have completed a tour of duty in the UK. Indefinite exclusion from the UK system may be available in certain circumstances (see **7.59**).

Bilateral agreements

9.54 The UK has bilateral social security agreements with a number of non-EC countries under which citizens of these countries working in the UK can obtain exemption from UK social security contributions in broadly the same manner as EC nationals (see **7.57**). Mere residence in the other country before coming to the UK will not suffice. There is normally the added requirement that the employee must not be ordinarily resident in the UK. Bilateral agreements also provide for payments of UK social security benefits to nationals of the other country, and for free medical treatment under the UK health scheme.

US expatriates

9.55   As indicated in **5.46**, there is a US/UK social security agreement under which employees seconded from one country to the other may remain within the home country social security system for up to 5 years. It is normally required that there is a continuing employment with an employer in the home country. For employees who are US citizens, a US employer may elect that they remain within the US social security system even though they are employed by an overseas subsidiary of the US employer. Where such an election is in force, the DSS treat employment by a UK subsidiary of the US employer as if it were a secondment, so that the exemption from UK contributions applies, assuming that the other conditions are satisfied.

Visas and work permits

9.56   As mentioned in **8.53**, nationals of EC member states do not require a visa to enter the UK nor a work permit in order to take an employment. Registration is necessary for a stay of longer than six months, in order to obtain a residence permit.

9.57   Non-EC nationals require work permits to take up employment in the UK. The employer should apply to the Department of Employment for a permit before the employee's arrival and must normally be able to demonstrate that reasonable efforts have been made to recruit a UK or EC national to fill the vacancy. Permits can normally be obtained for non-EC nationals. The application should be made by a UK employer. The permits are granted for a specific job and are subject to annual renewal. Any employment changes must be notified to the Department of Employment. After four years the Home Office may, on application, waive the time limit and grant permanent residence thereby enabling the employee to change jobs freely.

Appendices

Appendix 1
British Government Stocks

Interest tax free if held by individuals not ordinarily resident in the UK

12¾% Treasury Loan 1992
10½% Treasury Conv Stock 1992*
12½% Treasury Loan 1993
6% Funding Loan 1993
13¾% Treasury Loan 1993
14½% Treasury Loan 1994
9% Treasury Loan 1994
12¾% Treasury Loan 1995
9% Treasury Loan 1992/96
15¼% Treasury Loan 1996
13¼% Exchequer Loan 1996
13¼% Treasury Loan 1997
8¾% Treasury Loan 1997
6¾% Treasury Loan 1995/98
15½% Treasury Loan 1998
9½% Treasury Loan 1999
8% Treasury Loan 2002/06
5½% Treasury Stock 2008/12
7¾% Treasury Loan 2012/15
3½% War Loan 1952 or after

The list includes only those stocks not redeemed at 31 August 1991.

All the securities except those marked* are excluded property for IHT where held by persons not resident, ordinarily resident or domiciled in the UK.

Appendix 2
OECD model residence article

1 For the purposes of this Convention, the term 'resident of a Contracting State' means any person who, under the laws of that State, is liable to tax therein by reason of his domicile, residence, place of management or any other criterion of a similar nature. But this term does not include any person who is liable to tax in that State in respect only of income from sources in that State or capital situated therein.

2 Where by reason of the provisions of paragraph 1 an individual is a resident of both Contracting States, then his status shall be determined as follows:

(a) he shall be deemed to be a resident of the State in which he has a permanent home available to him; if he has a permanent home available to him in both States, he shall be deemed to be a resident of the State with which his personal and economic relations are closer (centre of vital interests);
(b) if the State in which he has his centre of vital interests cannot be determined, or if he has not a permanent home available to him in either State, he shall be deemed to be a resident of the State in which he has an habitual abode;
(c) if he has an habitual abode in both States or in neither of them, he shall be deemed to be a resident of the State of which he is a national;
(d) if he is a national of both States or of neither of them, the competent authorities of the Contracting States shall settle the question by mutual agreement.

3 Where by reason of the provisions of paragraph 1 a person other than an individual is a resident of both Contracting States, then it shall be deemed to be a resident of the State in which its place of effective management is situated.

Appendix 3
Useful addresses

Tax

General:

Any HM Inspector of Taxes office or PAYE enquiry office (see local telephone directory under 'Inland Revenue')

Claims Branch – Foreign Division

St Johns House,
Merton Road,
Bootle,
Merseyside L69 9BB
(tel: 051-922 6363)

Inspector of Foreign
Dividends
Superannuation Funds
Office

Lynwood Road
Thames Ditton
Surrey KT7 0DP
(tel: 081-398 4242)

Foreign Entertainers
Unit

5th Floor
City House
140 Edmund Street
Birmingham B3 2JH
(tel: 021-200 2616)

Social Security

International aspects

Department of Social Security, Overseas Branch, Newcastle upon Tyne NE98 1YX
(tel: 091-285 7111)

General

Any local Social Security office (see local telephone directory under 'Social Security')

Work permits

Before arrival in UK:

Application by UK employer to nearest Professional and Executive Recruitment Office or Jobcentre (see local telephone directory under 'Manpower Services Commission, Employment Services Division') or employment centre (see under 'Employment')

After arrival in UK:

Application by UK employer to:
Home Office,
Immigration and Nationality Department,
Lunar House,
Wellesley Road,
Croydon CR9 2BY
(tel: 081-686 0688)

General enquiries:
(Great Britain)

Department of Employment,
Overseas Labour Section,
Caxton House,
Tothill Street,
London SW1H 9NF
(tel: 071-273 3000)

(Northern Ireland)

Employment Permits Branch,
Netherleigh,
Massey Avenue,
Belfast BT4 2JS
(tel: 023-276 3244)

Immigration

General enquiries
(UK)

Home Office,
Immigration and Nationality Department,
Lunar House,
Wellesley Road,
Croydon CR9 2BY
(tel: 081-686 0688)

(Abroad)

Nearest British Embassy

Appendix 4
OECD model domicile article

Fiscal domicile

1 For the purposes of this Convention, the question whether a person at his death was domiciled in a Contracting State shall be determined according to the law of that State.

2 Where by reason of the provisions of paragraph 1 a person was domiciled in both Contracting States, then this case shall be determined in accordance with the following rules.

(a) He shall be deemed to have been domiciled in the Contracting State in which he had a permanent home available to him. If he had a permanent home available to him in both Contracting States, the domicile shall be deemed to be in the Contracting State with which his personal and economic relations were closest (centre of vital interests);

(b) If the Contracting State in which he had his centre of vital interest cannot be determined, or if he had not a permanent home available to him in either Contracting State, the domicile shall be deemed to be in the Contracting State in which he has an habitual abode;

(c) If he had an habitual abode in both Contracting States or in neither of them, the domicile shall be deemed to be in the Contracting State of which he was a national;

(d) If he was a national of both Contracting States or of neither of them, the competent authorities of the Contracting States shall settle the question by mutual agreement.

Appendix 5

UK paying agents: credit for foreign withholding tax

The following sets out the rates of withholding tax on foreign dividends for which credit may be given by UK paying agents.

Country	Dividends %	Interest %	Notes
Australia	15	10	bd
Austria	15	–	cd
Belgium	10	15	d
Canada	15	–	c
Denmark	15	–	cd
Finland	5	–	cd
France	–	10	df
Germany	15	–	cd
Israel	15	15	de
Jamaica	15	12.5	d
Japan	15	10	d
Kenya	15	15	e
Luxembourg	15	–	c
Namibia	12.5	–	ac
Netherlands	15	–	cd
New Zealand	15	15	
Norway	15	–	cd
Philippines	25	–	cd
South Africa	15	10	a
Spain	15	12	d
Swaziland	15	7.5	a
Sweden	5	–	cd
Switzerland	15	–	cd
Trinidad & Tobago	20	10	d
USA	15	–	cd
Zambia	15	10	d
Zimbabwe	20	10	e

Notes

a As the withholding tax is payable only on the proportion of the dividend which is attributable to the net profit derived in South Africa, Namibia or Swaziland, as appropriate, the rate may be less than that shown.
b The dividend withholding tax rate is nil where a foreign company derived not less than 90% of its income for each of its last three accounting periods before the dividend was paid from a business carried on by it in the UK.
c The authority to deduct UK tax at a reduced rate does not extend to interest.
d Tax may be withheld at a rate higher than that authorised for credit, the difference usually being refundable.

e In the case of certain approved enterprises the rate of tax deducted may be less than that shown.

f The authority to deduct UK tax at a reduced rate does not extend to dividends.

Appendix 6

Illustration of UK tax liability for expatriate executive

Total compensation package of salary £60,000 plus fully-expensed car, rented accommodation at £350 per week, and children's school fees of £5,000 per annum. UK tax year 1991/92.

	UK resident employer
Income	
Salary	£60,000
Accommodation	18,200
School fees	5,000
Company car and fuel (say)	6,400
Taxable compensation	89,600
Less:	
Personal allowance (married)	(5,015)
Net taxable income	84,585
UK income tax	£30,279
National insurance contributions (employee)	£ 1,636
Net spendable amount after tax	£28,085

Index